Underwater Forensics

by Gail B. Stewart

928 7483

8- 20½

LUCENT BOOKS
A part of Gale, Cengage Learning

GALE
CENGAGE Learning

Detroit • New York • San Francisco • New Haven, Conn • Waterville, Maine • London

GALE
CENGAGE Learning™

LIBRARY OF CONGRESS CATALOGING-IN-PUBLICATION DATA

Stewart, Gail B. (Gail Barbara), 1949-
  Underwater forensics / by Gail B. Stewart.
    p. cm. -- (Crime scene investigations)
  Includes bibliographical references and index.
  ISBN 978-1-4205-0214-5 (hardcover)
  1. Underwater crime investigation. 2. Crime scene searches.
  3. Police divers. I. Title.
  HV8080.D54S74 2010
  363.25--dc22

                                                    2009039383

Lucent Books
27500 Drake Rd.
Farmington Hills, MI 48331

ISBN-13: 978-1-4205-0214-5
ISBN-10: 1-4205-0214-X

Printed in the United States of America
1 2 3 4 5 6 7 14 13 12 11 10

Printed by Bang Printing, Brainerd, MN, 1st Ptg., 04/2010

Contents

Foreword

The popularity of crime scene and investigative crime shows on television has come as a surprise to many who work in the field. The main surprise is the concept that crime scene analysts are the true crime solvers, when in truth, it takes dozens of people, doing many different jobs, to solve a crime. Often, the crime scene analyst's contribution is a small one. One Minnesota forensic scientist says that the public "has gotten the wrong idea. Because I work in a lab similar to the ones on *CSI*, people seem to think I'm solving crimes left and right—just me and my microscope. They don't believe me when I tell them that it's the investigators that are solving crimes, not me."

Crime scene analysts do have an important role to play, however. Science has rapidly added a whole new dimension to gathering and assessing evidence. Modern crime labs can match a hair of a murder suspect to one found on a murder victim, for example, or recover a latent fingerprint from a threatening letter, or use a powerful microscope to match tool marks made during the wiring of an explosive device to a tool in a suspect's possession.

Probably the most exciting of the forensic scientist's tools is DNA analysis. DNA can be found in just one drop of blood, a dribble of saliva on a toothbrush, or even the residue from a fingerprint. Some DNA analysis techniques enable scientists to tell with certainty, for example, whether a drop of blood on a suspect's shirt is that of a murder victim.

While these exciting techniques are now an essential part of many investigations, they cannot solve crimes alone. "DNA doesn't come with a name and address on it," says the Minnesota forensic scientist. "It's great if you have someone in custody to match the sample to, but otherwise, it doesn't help.

That's the investigator's job. We can have all the great DNA evidence in the world, and without a suspect, it will just sit on the shelf. We've all seen cases with very little forensic evidence get solved by the resourcefulness of a detective."

While forensic specialists get the most media attention today, the work of detectives still forms the core of most criminal investigations. Their job, in many ways, has changed little over the years. Most cases are still solved through the persistence and determination of a criminal detective whose work may be anything but glamorous. Many cases require routine, even mind-numbing tasks. After the July 2005 bombings in London, for example, police officers sat in front of video players watching thousands of hours of closed-circuit television tape from security cameras throughout the city, and as a result were able to get the first images of the bombers.

The Lucent Books Crime Scene Investigations series explores the variety of ways crimes are solved. Titles cover particular crimes such as murder, specific cases such as the killing of three civil rights workers in Mississippi, or the role specialists such as medical examiners play in solving crimes. Each title in the series demonstrates the ways a crime may be solved, from the various applications of forensic science and technology to the reasoning of investigators. Sidebars examine both the limits and possibilities of the new technologies and present crime statistics, career information, and step-by-step explanations of scientific and legal processes.

The Crime Scene Investigations series strives to be both informative and realistic about how members of law enforcement—criminal investigators, forensic scientists, and others—solve crimes, for it is essential that student researchers understand that crime solving is rarely quick or easy. Many factors—from a detective's dogged pursuit of one tenuous lead to a suspect's careless mistakes to sheer luck to complex calculations computed in the lab—are all part of crime solving today.

"Everything's Different Now"

Ask most people to come up with a mental image of a crime scene, and they might think of a dark alley or the gang-infested streets of a big city. But talk to Dick Hagen, a special deputy to a Minnesota sheriff's office, and the first crime scene he thinks of is water. It could be the Mississippi River or one of the thousands of deep, cold lakes scattered throughout the state. Or it might be an ocean far from Minnesota—maybe a crystal blue cove in the Pacific. It might even be a shallow pond on the ninth hole of an exclusive country club's golf course.

It is in those places that Hagen, and thousands of police divers like him around the world, have discovered evidence of violent crimes that were all but invisible to most of the population. They have found the water-ravaged bodies of murder victims—many barely recognizable as human beings—as well as the guns, knives, and other weapons used to kill them. They have even discovered submerged vehicles driven or pushed into deep water by criminals concerned about clues the police could use to identify them.

"Come On, How Did You Do That?"

"When you think about it, it probably isn't that surprising that there are so many [underwater crime scenes], considering that the earth is what—like seventy percent water?" says Hagen. "Statistically, that would probably mean that there would be more stuff down under the water than other places, I guess."[1]

Dave, a diver for a Texas sheriff's department, agrees with Hagen but says water has a special draw for some criminals. "I think that it's so easy to think of a large body of water as being completely safe, as far as hiding weapons and other evidence," he says. "If a guy wants to ditch a knife or a gun he's used to kill someone, there is something about deep water that seems absolutely foolproof. I mean, no one's going to stumble upon that weapon, like they might if he hid it on land somewhere."[2]

He also believes that people think that evidence found under the water will be worthless. "They figure that if someone finds that gun, or knife, or whatever it is, all the trace [evidence] will have been washed off in the water. So many criminals are just floored when we pull some key piece of evidence out of a lake or a river and can connect it with him. They're like, 'Come on, how did you *do* that?'"[3]

The Way It Used to Be

Unfortunately, the assumption that very little can be learned from submerged evidence was accurate for many years. Looking back, experts like Florida State University underwater forensics expert Gregg Stanton are more than aware of how crimes went unsolved simply because no one knew the value of underwater forensics. Stanton says that such retrieval would be like a modern-day police detective "going to a crime scene [on land], stepping through the evidence, finding a body, grabbing it by the ankle, and dragging it out of the scene."[4]

But dismissing the possibility of underwater forensic evidence was common. For one thing, a submerged murder victim was often impossible to find. Unless a body washed ashore, the currents and depths of a river or ocean made it difficult to even conduct a murder investigation. And even when a body was discovered, the physical changes it had gone through from being in the water made identification difficult for medical examiners, let alone finding a cause of death.

It was assumed that blood, semen, and other bodily fluids that provide helpful clues in most crimes would wash away from a body and clothing in water. The same was true for any trace evidence such as hair or fibers that might provide investigators with important clues. Those could not have survived on the body while it was underwater. And what about the idea

A gun is recovered by a police diver. New technologies have made it easier for police to perform underwater forensics.

of getting important evidence like fingerprints from a weapon that had been sitting on the bottom of a lake for weeks? "If you suggested that when I started out, you would have been laughed right out of the room,"[5] says Don, a retired forensic technician from Michigan.

A Whole Different World

But in the twenty-first century, investigators say things have changed a lot. Many of the changes have been technological. For example, divers used to just estimate where a submerged vehicle or a body might be and then do their dives—often with little success. But new instruments now allow them to see what is under the water before they begin a dive.

"A lot of the time, we know we've got a body or a vehicle down there before we even send one of our guys in the water," says Hagen. "That's completely changed the way underwater searches work. Use your sonar from the boat and you can see what's under there—or what's not under there. You can't believe the time that saves."[6]

Other important advances have occurred in the modern forensics laboratory. New chemicals can help technicians process submerged weapons for fingerprints and other important evidence. Medical examiners have more tools available for learning not only the identity of a body, or even part of a body, that has been recovered in water but also for finding clues to the manner in which that person died.

Looking back on the way underwater evidence was once retrieved, some experts wince. No one can estimate how many crimes went unsolved. Says Ron, a Minnesota diver, "The thing is, very few clues were found, just because nobody expected there to be any. It was nobody's fault—divers just didn't know back then. But law enforcement has made huge strides, and all that's changed. There's so much more we can do now."[7]

CHAPTER ONE

"Cops with Swim Fins"

Many of the questions about a crime are answered in the forensic laboratory. Technicians use a variety of machines, chemicals, and scientific instruments to study evidence, and they often find evidence that reveals the identity of the person who committed the crime. But the first link in the chain of solving a crime involving water is the diver. The diver's job is to actually find and retrieve submerged evidence. "No doubt . . . the technicians in the lab work magic, but we're the ones who are able to give them something to work with," says Tony, a Florida diver. "And more and more, how we work that crime scene can either make or break a criminal case."[8]

The Eyes and Hands of the Police

They are called public safety divers, or police divers, and they have a wide range of duties. They are called in when any death—suspicious or not—occurs within a body of water. They recover the bodies of victims of boating and swimming accidents. But they are also the first responders to underwater crime scenes. They have the expertise to work these scenes—something regular police detectives cannot do.

"Our diving knowledge gives us the edge in this environment," says Tony. "I've heard someone refer to public service divers as 'cops with swim fins.' I guess that's right. I mean, I think you'd have a hard time naming another type of investigator or forensic tech who is risking his or her life each and every time just going to the crime scene. You can't do it."[9]

Hagen agrees, adding, "I think of us as an extension of both the detective and the crime lab technician," he says. "We've found that when it's an underwater job, it's a lot easier and less time consuming for us to do their jobs than it is to teach them to do what we do."[10]

"Pretty Much a Braille Method"

But it would be a mistake to envision the kind of underwater environment one sees on television, with crystal blue water and colorful fish swimming around. Most of the time, divers can see no more than 10 feet (3m) in front of them. And much of that time, divers do their work in what they refer to as "black water" conditions, or "nil viz," as divers in Britain call it. That means that much of the time they can see only a few inches in front of their facemasks, and often not even that much.

By the Numbers

4,000

Approximate number of drowning deaths in the United States yearly.

Police divers must frequently perform forensic tasks in conditions where seeing is difficult.

"You ask me, and I say it's just as well," says Craig, a diver from Illinois.

There's a lot of really gross stuff down there, especially the rivers. I mean, there are cars down there, shopping carts, tons of garbage people have thrown in. It really doesn't matter what type of water you're diving in, but I think rivers are among the worst. Besides the pollution, which makes the water oily and kind of soupy, when a diver goes down deep—which is where we work—you're stirring up a lot of silt from the bottom, which makes it impossible to see anything at all. So I'm used to holding my hand up in front [of my facemask] and not seeing anything at all, and that's probably for the best.[11]

The lack of visibility means that divers rely on their sense of touch—working slowly, doing fingertip searches inch by inch along the bottom of the body of water. Their experience enables them to recognize very quickly what objects they encounter, in the same way a blind person does. Former police diver Bill Chandler says the comparison is apt for black water divers, calling such searches "pretty much a Braille method."[12]

The Rock Garden

But how does a diver locate an important piece of evidence when visibility is basically zero? "Training, training, and more training," says Hagen. "That's the only way to do it. I mean, find a clip [from an automatic weapon] underwater? Try doing that with your eyes closed, in a river where there are a million things on the bottom, when you've got diving gloves on—you absolutely have to use gloves, because of all the razor wire, broken bottles and other sharp stuff in the water. But my divers learn to do it."[13]

Hagen says it is vitally important for divers to learn to recognize things by touch.

Scrubbing Down

There are a lot of different underwater environments, but according to veteran police diver Dick Hagen, the shallow ponds are the worst:

> My divers hate those little ponds—whether they're the ones on golf courses or those ponds over by railroad tracks, where they load and unload stuff—you can imagine all the junk that's in those ponds. After doing dives in those ponds, we call the local fire department down to decontaminate our guys. They get hosed down, and then we go after the divers with this biodegradable soap called Simple Green that we put in an apple sprayer. And we scrub them down with pot brushes.
>
> Golf courses have geese, and that can be bad for divers. Those ponds are full of goose poop and fertilizers, and all the chemicals they use to keep the course green. But it's murder on my guys—lots of stuff that can damage the eyes and skin. So we are careful to do that scrubbing every time we dive in a situation like that.

Dick Hagen, personal interview, Medina, MN, April 10, 2009.

A diver emerges from a contaminated pond after searching for a body. He will need to be hosed down and scrubbed with biodegradable soap to insure his health.

Just a couple of days ago, we were in the river looking for a clip from a weapon that had been used in a crime. A couple days before that we were searching for shell casings. And using your eyes just wasn't an option—the water was like soup. My divers need to get really comfortable with finding a clip, or a shell casing that's been ditched in the water—because there are a lot of them down there. That's where the bad guys toss their stuff a lot of the time.[14]

Forensic divers must be able to perform delicate tasks underwater while using protective gloves.

He trains the divers using a swimming pool that he calls his "rock garden." After adding a large bucket of granite chips, he throws in other debris—chunks of rope, pieces of pipe, and other things that divers often encounter on the river bottom. "I'll add railroad spikes, too, because they are the same general size and shape as automatic weapon clips,"

he says. "[Finding a clip or casing is] a real challenge for those divers, whose masks are taped over—so they've got to rely on touch alone." How long does it take divers to become proficient at that? "It takes about a year and a half for them to get *really* good at it," says Hagen. "And even after that, we continue training."[15]

The Equipment

Training is also necessary to become used to the equipment divers require. In fact, everything about the dive—from the tanks containing their air supply, to the diving suits they wear, to their communication devices—are checked and rechecked before they go into the water.

"Safety is everything in this business," says Michigan diver Al Rogers. "It's vital to make sure everything is working before every single dive. My first diving instructor always told us, 'You guys only need to check your equipment if you plan on breathing during your dive.' So yeah, we check our stuff constantly."[16]

Besides making sure the breathing apparatus is in good working order and the tank has a good supply of air, divers also check their diving suits for rips that might let water in. "That's a big deal, because the kind of water we dive in, you wouldn't want anywhere close to your skin," says Rogers. "We do all our dives in dry suits, not the standard rubber suits scuba divers use. For one thing, rubber suits don't keep you warm enough if you're diving in water less than fifty-five degrees. We do dives in water a lot colder than that—even under ice sometimes—so a rubber suit would be a deal breaker for us."[17]

Police divers do not wear typical scuba masks that cover only the nose and eyes for the same reasons they prefer the dry suit. The water that contains garbage, bacteria, and a host

Because the water contains contaminants and bacteria, forensic divers must wear dry suits and protective headgear to minimize their exposure.

of parasites would cause more trouble on the sensitive skin of a diver's face—especially the nose and eyes—than on the rest of his body. That is why the majority of divers wear full face masks, just like the ones firefighters wear.

Staying in Touch

Built into a diver's full face mask is communications gear—an earpiece and microphone that allows him or her to maintain contact with the rest of the dive crew in the boat above. "Electronic communication is really helpful, and makes things easier," says Hagen. "But we still teach the old fashioned way, too—rope signals. One tug on a rope means something, two tugs means something else. I'll tell you, rope signals are good on a couple of levels. One, obviously, is if your comm [communications] line fails, something goes wrong with the electronics. Even if that happens, you can still communicate with your tender."[18]

In some cases, Hagen says, he actually prefers to use rope signals, because reporters and photographers often use boom mikes to try to listen in on police communications at the scene of a crime or accident. "I knew they're doing their job—they want to know what's going on, so they can get their photo, or their story," he says. "But for us it's a pain."[19]

Hagen reasons that some things divers encounter should not be publicly viewed. "I remember deliberately dropping an airplane back in the river because there were TV people on the bank 20 feet [6m] away," he says.

> The reason I did that was because we had a body hanging out of the windshield. Nobody needs to see that. It's enough that we have to, but it's not doing anyone any good to show those images. Plus, you think about the family. So no, I told the sergeant, just get them out of here, and I'll bring the plane up, but not until they're gone. I'm the instructor, you know, so I've got a certain amount of clout, I guess."[20]

Primary, BUD, and 90 Percent

Whether recovering a crashed airplane, looking for a body, or searching for a weapon used in a crime, divers have a very rigid system for their mission. As police divers, they usually do not dive in pairs, called a "buddy system," as recreational divers do. "We always dive one at a time," says Hagen. "Each diver who goes down has what we call a tender, the guy holding the tether that is connected to the diver. 'Dope on a rope,' we call it," he says, smiling, and adds, "By the way, when I say 'guys,' I mean both men and women divers."[21]

The tenders are as important to the mission as divers are and receive almost the same kind of training as divers do. "Tenders are the last ones to look at you before you dive," says Hagen. "They look you over very carefully, make sure your equipment is in good order, check you out, turn you around and check the back, too. Like your mom making sure you've got your mittens and warm hat on before you go out in the snow, you know?"[22]

Most police dive teams have three divers in the boat, in various stages of readiness. "Primary is the one first in," explains Hagen.

The next one is BUD, which stands for backup diver. Then there's the one we call the 90 Percent. He's just a guy sitting in a chair on the boat. He's called 90 Percent because he doesn't have all the gear on, like BUD does. But all 90 Percent's gear is checked and ready for him to put on when need be. Otherwise, he's got his dry suit on, and he's pretty close to being ready—90 percent ready.[23]

Having three divers is helpful, says Hagen, for if Primary diver has a problem—such as an equipment malfunction—another diver is always ready to fill in. "When BUD goes into the water, he deals with the problem with Primary, who then comes out of the water," he says. "Then when BUD goes in, 90 Percent moves up a chair, becoming BUD. And Primary is at the back of the line. If BUD were to have a problem, then 90 Percent goes down to help, and BUD comes out. It's a backup system, so a dive can keep going even if you've got two divers with problems—and believe me, it does happen."[24]

Even if a diver does not have a problem, Hagen says, he or she needs to come out of the water after twenty minutes or so. "Every team has its own rules," he says, "and that's one of ours. See, after twenty minutes or so, it's hard to concentrate. Remember, you can't see anything. You can imagine, you're

By the Numbers

7 MILES [11 KM]

The depth in feet of the deepest trenches on the ocean floor.

just groping, concentrating really hard. After twenty minutes, it's easy to lose your edge, and that's not good for anybody. So the next diver has to be ready to go."[25]

Dangers Below the Surface

Planning for problems is an important part of being a public safety diver, simply because the stakes are so high. An accident or mistake for a police officer usually means that he or she needs to spend extra time and energy correcting it. When a police diver has an accident or makes a mistake, it can result in injury or even death.

One Federal Bureau of Investigation (FBI) diver found this out during a training exercise that could have been disastrous. He became entangled in some rope underwater. In this particular case, he was using traditional scuba gear rather than a full face mask. When the diver reached down to free himself

A constant danger for a forensics diver is becoming entangled in a crime scene debris field.

from the rope, his regulator (the mouthpiece through which a diver breathes underwater) caught on some fishing line, and it was pulled from his mouth.

Even though the water in which he was diving was relatively shallow, he would have died had he not been closely monitored by his supervisors. "You get in a situation like that, when you lose your regulator suddenly, you don't have time to even take a breath," says Craig. "It's one of the scariest things that can happen to you underwater."[26]

"That's why divers now carry shears with them," says Hagen. "You don't know what you're going to run into down there. Entanglement from ropes, fishing line, wires—any of that stuff can catch on the diver or his equipment. That's probably the number one most common danger for a diver."[27]

Pressure and the Diver's Body

A dangerous problem for divers who work in very deep water is decompression sickness, often called "the bends." This occurs when a diver surfaces too quickly, and nitrogen in the blood forms bubbles. These bubbles can cause problems by blocking blood flow to tissues and organs. Mild bubbling of nitrogen in the diver's knees or elbows can cause severe pain, but high levels of bubbling can result in paralysis, lung and heart problems, and even death. To prevent that from happening, divers surface very slowly, stopping along the way at several points to allow nitrogen that has built up in their bodies to leave gradually.

Even very experienced divers can be at risk. In May 2009 *National Geographic* photographer Carl Spencer was diving off the coast of Greece, taking photos of the *Britannic*, sister ship of the legendary *Titanic*. The *Britannic* had sunk in 1916 and was to be the subject of a story in the magazine. But after experiencing a medical problem nearly 300 feet (90m) under the water, experts say that Spencer came to the surface too quickly without stopping at various points along the way to decompress gradually. As a result, the thirty-seven-year-old photographer died from severe decompression sickness.

Emotional Distress

But while physical risks are inherent in their work, other problems are equally as dangerous. "This can be a great job," says Craig,

> but it can also be the worst. A big part of the job is recovery of bodies, and emotionally that can really take a toll. And when I say "bodies," I use the term loosely, because they are often partial bodies, or if they are intact, they are in terrible shape. Critters under the water, and just the passage of time can cause some pretty startling decomposition. And even for divers, who see that on a pretty regular basis, it can make a human body pretty difficult to look at.[28]

One of the most difficult situations for London diver Marion Dutton occurred after the London bombings in July 2005, when terrorists bombed subway trains in the city. Because she is trained in both underwater and confined spaces searching, Dutton was required to do both when she crawled under a bombed train. "I was crawling through body fluids under the train for hours in the pitch dark," she remembers. "People were literally evaporated—I found pairs of earrings with the backs still on."[29]

Many divers try to keep an emotional distance from the things they witness while they are doing such work. Otherwise, they say, being overwhelmed by the sadness of the situation would be too easy. "You don't tend to talk much about how you feel," Dutton says. "You try not to connect."[30]

A Wrenching Recovery

But that can be extremely difficult in certain situations. One of the worst for some South Carolina divers was a case that occurred in October 1994. Susan Smith, a young mother of two little boys, was distraught because she had fallen in love with a man who did not want her children.

A police diver tells other officers that he has found the car containing the bodies of Susan Smith's two murdered children.

She drove to the steep edge of a boat ramp at John D. Long Lake in Union, South Carolina. With the toddlers strapped securely in their car seats, she released the emergency brake and watched the car roll into the deep water. To make sure that she would not be blamed for their deaths, Smith pretended to be frantic. She told police that she had been carjacked by a man who had let her go but not her sons. Crying and pleading with police to find her sons, Smith quickly became a very sympathetic national news story.

As police and community volunteers searched around the clock for any sign of the car, police were becoming suspicious of Smith's story. Why would any carjacker, they wondered, allow an adult to go free but hold on to two little boys? Finally, as they continued to interview her, Smith broke down, admitted that she was responsible, and told police where the car had rolled into the lake. Police divers were quickly called to the scene. Although it took awhile to locate the car, which had settled into the silt at the bottom of the lake, divers found it upside down, the bodies of the two children still inside.

"Veteran diver Steve Morrow, stood on the banks and cried," writes *Time* reporter Nancy Gibbs. "'There's no way to be thick-skinned about something like this,' he said. 'When it's an accidental death you can deal with it a little better, but knowing that someone could deliberately. . . .' his voice trails off. When he got home that night, Morrow says, he crawled into bed with his little boy. 'I just had to hold him for awhile.'"[31]

"I Was Done"

Divers are never certain when they are called to a scene if the death is suspicious, but even bodies that are believed to be accident victims can be emotionally difficult for them. "I found a young kid in Lake Minnetonka, eleven years old," says Hagen. "His name was Kevin, and I'll never forget him. It was a long time ago, but I remember it like it happened this morning. I was in 45 feet [13.7m] of water," he remembers, "and actually stepped on his tennis shoe. I knew it was a shoe just by the feel. I reached back, and there was an ankle. I grabbed him by the ankle, and brought him up."[32]

Hagen says that when he got to the surface, he realized the boy's head had almost been severed by the propeller of the boat he had been in. "And I looked at his face and he looked just like my wife's nephew. Okay, well, I was done that day. I was done. Through. I just needed to get away, sit by myself. So I did. And after a bit, I was ready to go back to work, do my job. In all my years of diving, that hit me the hardest."[33]

Working with the Family

Bill Chandler, a police diver for many years, says that establishing a connection with the family of the person they were searching for used to help him. "Whether it's a criminal investigation or an accidental drowning—and a lot of times you don't know at the time you're doing the search—it helps to have the family connection. They need to be kept in the loop—what you're doing, what's the status of the search."[34]

He says it makes no difference if the dive team has found the victim or not. "They just want to be included," he explains. "Even if we haven't found anything yet. But you treat them well, you know, you try to take care of them. For whatever reason, I was the one talking to the family, but taking care of them actually seemed to help me, to keep me focused as a diver and take my mind off how it was affecting me personally."[35]

Chandler says that connection can sometimes last well beyond the crisis. "I have a family that still sends me a Christmas card every year," he says. "I recovered the body of their father.

Solved: A Seventy-Two-Year-Old Mystery

On July 3, 1929, Russell and Blanch Warren of rural Washington disappeared on their way home from buying a washing machine. Neither their car nor their bodies were ever found, but some people wondered if their car had gone off the road and into deep Lake Crescent at a curve that had no guardrail. Their two little boys were devastated and felt that their parents had abandoned them.

But in April 2002 a National Park Service search team aided by volunteer divers solved the mystery. A local man had always been interested in stories of the Warren disappearance and got the help of a side-scan sonar expert to search the lake. After locating an object on sonar that he figured was the washing machine, Ralston plotted the location on a GPS [Global Positioning System] and alerted divers. He was just as surprised as they when it turned out to be the car. "There are chrome parts that are just as shiny as the day they were made," said one of the divers. Though no sign of the bodies was found, the great-grandchildren of the missing couple were relieved that they had an answer at last.

Quoted in Kristin Dizon, "Car in Lake May Solve 72-Year-Old Mystery," *Seattle Post-Intelligencer*, April 15, 2002, p. A1.

It took almost ten days, and I was meeting with them every day, answering all their questions. It's been many years since that case, but there's still that connection we have."[36]

Police divers have a lot of responsibility—from being fit and comfortable with the equipment they use, to being able to "see" underwater evidence with only their fingertips, to understanding the emotional and physical risks inherent in the job. And all of those things become critically important each time they are summoned to an underwater scene.

CHAPTER TWO

Finding the Underwater Evidence

When the divers receive a call, they are often unsure whether they will be responding to a crime or to an accident. A man's body that washed up on the shore of a lake or riverbank might be an accidental drowning victim. But it is also possible that he was the victim of something more sinister. Divers say it is crucial to keep an open mind when they first arrive at the scene.

Doug, a volunteer Michigan police diver, says that occurred to him several years ago when he and his crew were called to a small lake on a July afternoon. Two men had been fishing in a boat, and one of the men had fallen into the water and drowned:

> They'd been doing some drinking out there, I guess. His friend called it in quick, and we were able to retrieve the body pretty fast. And it was probably an accident—there was nothing to indicate there was anything else. But you know, it's funny how we always assume drownings are accidents. I remember reading somewhere—and it's true—that if a similar situation occurred on land—two guys were up on a roof and one ended up on the pavement below— police would be all over that case as a possible homicide. But water just changes things somehow. The bottom line is that we've got to go where the facts tell us. And that means we need to be as thorough about investigating water calls as we are about police calls on dry land.[37]

The Difficulty of Witnesses

The first step in any police investigation is to locate the evidence, and investigations on or under water are no different. If it is a gun, a vehicle that went into the water, or a body, police divers hope that someone witnessed the event. But as they have learned, even multiple eyewitnesses can have difficulty when trying to pinpoint a location in water.

Emergency personnel recover a drowning victim from a lake. Divers say it is critical to keep an open mind when investigating drownings.

"For one thing, it's hard because you don't have the same perception of distance," says Doug. "You don't have the markers like on land—trees, buildings, stuff like that. So when you ask a witness how far out from shore something happened, a lot of times, they're just not sure. Water is deceptive."[38]

Often police divers will have a deputy out in a boat to give a visual clue to the witness. "Having that boat out there helps," says Doug.

We first make sure that witness is back to the spot she was when she saw the event—whether it was a body going down [into the water], the gun being thrown, or whatever occurred. And then we get her to tell us when that deputy's boat is close to the spot where it happened. When she tells us that yeah, that's pretty close, we drop a buoy at that location. Not every witness will come up with the same exact location, so we'll drop a number of buoys. But hopefully we'll have a pretty good idea of where to begin our dive—at least the general area.[39]

To help locate a drowning victim, investigators often place buoys and flags in the water to mark locations given to them by eyewitnesses.

A good witness can save many frustrating hours of searching. A prime example occurred near the Riker Island Detention

Center in New York City in the late 1990s. A prisoner was able to escape and leap into the East River, hoping to swim to freedom. He underestimated the swift current of the river, however, and quickly went under the raging water.

A guard at the prison saw it happen, and while it was too late to save the escaped prisoner, the guard was able to tell divers exactly where the man went down—information that New York Police Department (NYPD) diver John Harkins says helped

By the Numbers

25

The percentage that the average witness underestimates distance over water.

them find the body on the second pass through the area. "I was glad," says Harkins. "This could have been one of those situations where we could have been out there all day. This emphasizes how important it is to get a good witness."[40]

Clues at the Water's Edge

In a great many cases, police find important clues that help them in the underwater search even before they enter the water. That is what happened in 2007 after Egyptian immigrant Mohamed Mahrous was killed in a Ravenswood, West Virginia, park near the Ohio River. It was obvious that Mahrous had died from a blow to the head, but at first police were unsure of what the killer had used as a weapon.

"The early autopsy results showed that it was some kind of hammer," recalls Ravenswood police chief Paul Hesson.

> The indentations in the skull were round and smooth. If a pipe or some other hard heavy object had been used, the indentation would have had a different shape. So that gave us an idea of what we were looking for. And the size of the indentation showed us that it was a big hammer, like maybe a three-pound sledge hammer, like one a pipe fitter would use.[41]

Hesson says that the police did a thorough search along the riverbank, believing the killer had probably thrown the hammer into the water. "What they found was really helpful," he says.

> There was a white plastic bag—like the kind you get when you go to the store—with blood on it. We figured that maybe the killer had concealed the hammer in the bag as he approached the victim, and he swung the hammer still in the bag, which accounted for the blood. Anyway, it gave us a good idea of where the killer had most likely been standing when he threw the hammer into the water.[42]

The next step, says Hesson, was to find a similar hammer and get an idea of how far one could throw it from that spot. "That's just what we did," he says. "One of my officers hurled one in from that spot on the riverbank, and that gave our divers an idea of where they should start searching."[43]

The Best Eyewitnesses of All

In a surprising number of cases, the criminals themselves provide specific information about the location of submerged evidence. In December 2007 burglars stole more than $800,000 worth of coins and jewelry from a Columbus, Ohio, home. Several members of the burglary ring were caught and admitted to police that they had thrown the jewelry into the water when they believed they were about to be apprehended. They offered to tell police divers where they threw the items they had stolen.

"It's called a plea bargain," explains Jon Corbett, an Illinois attorney. "The suspects are basically bargaining with the police, making a deal. They are willing to give the police information—in this case, about how divers can recover the valuables for the victim. In return, they are promised a somewhat lighter sentence than they would get if they had refused to cooperate."[44]

Police divers in Indiana received similar help in nailing down the details of a bloody attack on a young pizza delivery woman in September 2008. After an accomplice devised the plan—placing a phony hundred-dollar order for deluxe pizzas to be delivered to an empty house—the other two waited in the bushes until the delivery woman, twenty-one-year-old Samantha Wilson-Sayre, showed up. When she did, they beat her with a metal bar, took the pizzas, and went home to eat them.

Wilson-Sayre survived the brutal beating, however, and was able to describe her attackers to police. When the men were caught, one admitted his part in the crime immediately and offered to show police where they could find important evidence submerged in the nearby Deep River. He claimed that he had thrown not only the metal pipe into the water but also his shoes, which were covered in pizza sauce. He had worried that he would be caught and was anxious to get rid of any evidence that might point to his guilt. Helped by his specific directions, police divers were able to retrieve both the weapon and the shoes from the murky river, and the man received a lesser sentence than the others involved.

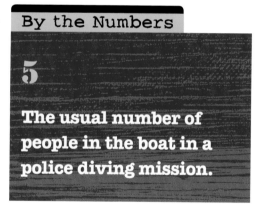

By the Numbers

5

The usual number of people in the boat in a police diving mission.

Making a Plan

Just knowing the general area where a piece of evidence is submerged is not enough to begin the dive, however. Once they know the area in which they will be searching, divers first prepare a plan. "We don't just hop in the water and look around," says Hagen. "We have to have a strategy before we dive. There are a number of different ways to search, and it all depends on what we're looking for, the depth of the water, and the conditions we'll be diving in."[45]

Sometimes, if the evidence is believed to be in shallow water, a diver may decide an arc search is best. The tender is on land with a long tether to the diver. The diver does his search in an arc pattern. When he gets to the end of the arc, the tender ties a knot in the rope, and the diver begins the arc closer to shore. Each time he reaches the end of the arc, the tender ties a new knot. Gradually, the diver comes closer and closer to shore, until he either finds the evidence or is convinced that he can eliminate that area.

Another method frequently used is called the Jackstay search. It involves two weights with a long rope line between them. The diver keeps one hand on the rope and slowly moves from one weight to the other, using his other hand to feel along the bottom. When he gets to the end of the rope, he moves the weight 2 feet [.6m] over, turns around, and heads back toward the first weight. When he gets there, he moves that weight, and so on. So that the crew in the boat can see the progress of the diver, a float is attached to each weight.

Investigators discuss the search pattern they will use at a nearby riverbank to locate a drowning victim.

"The Jackstay is a pretty important search pattern, because it works well when the water is murky and you can't see anything," says Craig, an Illinois diver. "And most divers can tell you, that's the majority of their cases—black water. You're basi-

Cadaver Dogs

More and more rescue diving teams have found success with cadaver dogs. These dogs specialize in the scents of dead human bodies. People who are alive have certain chemicals in their bodies that protect the lining of the stomach and other organs. When a person dies, those chemicals are no longer produced. That allows bacteria to invade those organs, which causes a faint smell. With a nose more than a thousand times stronger than a human, a cadaver dog can ride in the front of a boat and alert his handler when he detects that smell coming from deep underwater.

Cadaver dogs can detect decomposition odors underwater.

cally groping and feeling, rather than eyeballing. Jackstay lets you keep track of where you're going, so you don't miss spots. It's a good search for weapons, ammunition clips, and smaller pieces of evidence. But we've found [submerged] bodies using the Jackstay, too."[46]

Technology Helps

Divers also rely on technology when no witnesses can tell them where evidence may be submerged. Handheld metal detectors can help a diver find guns, knives, and other evidence made of metal. These are light and easy for divers to use, and because they can be programmed to vibrate, rather than emit a beep or flash a light to alert the user when they detect the presence of metal, they can be effective tools in black water conditions.

"Even better, they really save time when you're searching in conditions where you've got so much muck on the bottom of a lake that stuff sinks down into it," says Chandler. "You can put your hand down to the bottom and sink your hand down into your armpit and still not touch bottom. So guns and other things that are heavy will sink down into it, deeper and deeper over time. So in those situations, your search can be even slower. The metal detector can help a lot."[47]

Chandler remembers looking for a gun after a homicide in a suburb of Minneapolis. "We kind of had an idea of the general area where the gun was," he says. "The guy had thrown it from the car into the lake as he was driving away from the scene, so we knew it was close by. We were using a grid to search—we make it out of PVC pipe, just a three-foot by three-foot [.9m by .9m] template we can put down under the water. Each time we finish searching within the grid area, we move it and start a search over again."[48]

Chandler says he was nearing the end of his dive and was not having much success. "I was running low on air," he says,

> and I was just going to finish that particular grid before I went back up. I was using the metal detector, and I was getting lots of hits—mostly pop cans and stuff like that. I was just going along, scanning. I'd get a

> ### By the Numbers
>
> # 150 (46м)
>
> **Depth that cadaver dogs can detect a body underwater.**

hit, reach down—okay, another can, throw it over my shoulder, and keep scanning. And then I got another hit, and reached down, picked it up and was going to throw what I thought was another can over my shoulder and realized it was the gun, partially buried under the bottom! So yeah, those detectors can help a lot.[49]

A police diver uses a metal detector to find a weapon buried in the sediment.

More Advanced Technology

Sometimes divers need to look for evidence in much deeper water, such as in the ocean or a very deep lake. One of the most valuable instruments for this type of search is called side-scan sonar. It consists of a torpedo-shaped device—usually about 4 feet (1.2m) long—that is dragged behind the boat. The device uses sound waves, or impulses (often called "pings"), to detect underwater objects as it moves over the ocean floor. These pings bounce off the objects and return to the instrument, which feeds them into a computer on the boat. The computer takes these returned sound waves and processes them into an image of whatever objects are on the bottom.

It was side-scan sonar that enabled the FBI to begin a murder case in California in 2006. At least five wealthy businesspeople—most of them Russian immigrants—had been kidnapped in the Los Angeles area. Their families were notified of the abductions and told that if they did not pay the sizable ransom money, their loved ones would be killed.

Even though the ransoms were paid, the kidnappers did not release the victims, and law enforcement feared the worst. But without bodies to prove any murders had taken place, investigators had few options. However, when a fisherman and his family found a body washed up on the shore of a deep reservoir in Yosemite National Park, it was identified as one of the hostages. The case had turned deadly, and law enforcement officials assumed that the other bodies had probably been dumped in the same lake.

And that is exactly what had happened. Using side-scan sonar, experts located two more bodies under a bridge in 350 feet (106.7m) of water. Two others were located by the sonar under another bridge in the same reservoir, in 250 feet (76.2m) of water. One witness, who came forward in a plea bargain,

Sinking, then Floating

In most cases, a dead body will sink to the bottom as the lungs fill with water. Even if drowning did not cause the death, water will eventually get into the lungs. However, as the body begins to decompose, or break down, bacteria spread, creating gases. As the body fills with gas, it eventually floats to the surface.

was able to supply information about the murderers, and a dangerous criminal ring was destroyed.

Looking for the Car

A murder case in 1990 called for a different sort of technology. Police were almost certain that a Kansas City drug dealer named Tony Emery had killed a woman named Christine Elkins. Elkins, who had become addicted to drugs, had agreed to be a witness in a court case when Emery was arrested. Before she had a chance to do so, she disappeared, and police feared that Emery had killed her to prevent her from testifying. Though police tried for years to solve the case, Elkins's body was never found, and as a result, Emery could not be charged with the murder.

Six years later, however, an informant came forward and told police that Emery did indeed kill Elkins by beating her with a blackjack and putting her in the trunk of her own car.

The side-scan sonar (pictured) is one of the new technologies being used for deep-water forensic searching.

Emery and an accomplice then sank the car in the Missouri River. But since that time, the river had flooded its banks. Even though divers knew the general area where the two men had sunk the car initially, it would be very difficult to find. The river's current was dangerously fast—as much as 8 miles (13km) per hour—and even heavy objects like cars and trucks could travel a long way before settling in the muck at the bottom. Besides, the river in that general area was 1,000 feet (304.8m) across—a great deal of river to search.

Experts thought that a magnetometer would be just the thing to help. Initially developed to help the military locate underwater mines and unexploded torpedoes and to help geologists find likely sources of iron ore, the magnetometer measures tiny amounts of iron in the earth's magnetic field. (Unlike a metal detector, the magnetometer reacts only to iron and steel.) The instrument, which can be towed from a boat, gives off readings that are then plotted on a screen. Any unusually large metallic reading would be noted by the magnetometer operator. Police hoped that it could help find a large 1983 Oldsmobile in the Missouri River.

"He's Got It! He's Got It!"

Magnetometer experts in the boat were able to map out six or seven possibilities—areas where a car could be submerged. However, they could not know if any of these areas contained cars—and if they did, whether one would be that particular car with Missouri license plate B6E652. The next morning the divers went into the water at the first site, hoping to find out. They found a car, but it was the wrong make.

As a safety precaution for divers at the second site, which was farther from shore, a 1,000-pound (453.6kg) weight attached to a cable and buoy was dropped nearby from a coast guard ship. "The idea," says researcher Steve Jackson, "was that the divers could hang on to the cable to reach the bottom. However, the current was so strong that even the large buoy was dragged under."[50]

A magnetometer similar to this one was used to find Christine Elkins's submerged car seven years after she was murdered.

Instead, divers decided to strap on heavy weights that would keep them more stable in the current. The first two were unable to find anything at all at the site. The third diver was luckier. Through his communications gear, he told the boat crew that he was sure he found a two-door car, though because of the murky water, he was unable to see. He did a "swim-around," using his hands to feel the surface of the vehicle, and he was able to remove one of the license plates.

The crew in the boat, writes Jackson, was very nervous during the short time it took for the diver to surface. Was it the right car? When he came out of the water, one of the crew yelled, "B-six-E-six-five-two! He's got it! He's got it!"[51] The car had been found, and a seven-year search had ended.

Just Beginning

It is not surprising that investigators are delighted when an important piece of evidence is discovered by divers. They know the evidence may be crucial in explaining how that crime occurred.

"The evidence has value because it may prove whether or not a particular individual committed the crime," says Ellen, a New York crime lab technician. "You want to examine the remains of the body brought up from underwater, you want to examine the gun, or the knife, or the vehicle. Every tiny bit of evidence we can find can help police build a case, so that they will hopefully be able to bring a criminal to justice."[52]

On the other hand, while investigators know that the discovery of evidence is important, they also understand that finding a body, a weapon, or a vehicle submerged in the water is only the first link in a very long chain.

CHAPTER THREE

Clues from a Water Gun

The moment a submerged weapon is located, the diver's job goes to a new level, from search to recovery. A definite method needs to be followed in bringing the "water gun," as investigators and forensic workers refer to it, up to the waiting boat. If that method is not followed exactly, experts say, it can make a difference later.

"It's really no different from a gun find on land," says Craig.

Say a man has been shot outside a club on a street downtown, and the gun's there on the pavement next to the body. A police officer who drives up to the scene can't just pick up that gun and handle it. Everybody who's ever watched TV knows that. There's evidence that could be destroyed. Well, police divers follow the same rules. We have to be very careful with it—how it's retrieved. Otherwise there's a problem down the road when the case gets to court.[53]

Bringing It Up

A big reason for the rules divers follow is that any gun (or knife, for that matter) that has been submerged in water will change the moment it comes into contact with the air. The metal will begin to oxidize, or rust—and the process is rapid. "If you were to bring a gun up out of a lake, let's say—just bring it and hand it off to a guy in the boat, it would start rusting immediately," says Craig. "It's pretty amazing—it's king of like time-lapse photography—it literally rusts right in front of your eyes. Oxidation like that will completely eat [the gun] up, so it will be useless for the lab techs."[54]

Today's divers know that the way to prevent oxidation from occurring is to make sure the gun does not come into contact with the air. "I'll tell you the way we do it," says Hagen.

When divers recover a submerged weapon, they transport it in water to the crime lab to protect the evidence from oxidation.

The diver who finds the gun stays down there with it, while he lets the boat know. Then BUD—remember, the Backup Diver—gets involved. He grabs a Ziploc baggie—just your regular old plastic bag from the grocery store. On it, he writes the date, the ICR [incoming call number of the case], whatever. Then BUD sticks his hand in there and holds it open, and goes down to the diver who found the gun. Then Primary Diver drops it in the bag.[55]

Hagen says it is also important for Primary Diver to put some of the mud or sand from the bottom of the lake in the bag. "That's like a control," he explains. "If any material is found inside the barrel of the gun, the techs can compare it to the [lake's mud] we've just put in the bag. If it matches, then they know it came from the lake. If it doesn't—if it's some other type of soil—where did this stuff come from? You see? It can maybe lead to something when they get that to the lab."[56]

The divers surface with the gun, and once back to the boat, they seal the bag (which is too hard to do in black water conditions with gloves on). The bagged gun is placed in an evidence bucket on the boat, which is sealed, too, using red evidence tape. "The thing we're always aware of is the chain of custody," says Chandler.

> That's why we label everything that we bring up from underwater. That's why every time a piece of evidence is transferred from one person to another, we've got to sign. If I bring a gun up in a bag, and give it to the guy in the boat, we both sign that we've been in possession of the gun. Then when the lab gets it, they sign, too. That's for when the case goes to court. Everything's got to be documented.[57]

Into the Lab

When the recovered gun is transferred to the crime lab, technicians evaluate it. In some cases, material is found in the barrel of the gun. Called blowback, it may contain blood, bone fragments, or hair from the shooting victim. Many people are surprised that blowback is still evident in a submerged weapon. "You might think it would wash out underwater," says Hagen. "And if mishandled by whoever finds the gun, it probably would. But water can also act like plug—keeping material inside the barrel."[58]

43

Any material found in the barrel is carefully removed and sent to technicians who evaluate trace evidence. If hair is found, it might be matched to a sample of the victim's hair. If bits of bone, blood, or tissue are involved, technicians can test them for DNA. Trace evidence can be very valuable, establishing a link from that particular gun to a particular victim of a shooting.

Sometimes even a submerged weapon may have a fingerprint on it. "Very unlikely for a fingerprint to survive underwater on the surface of the gun," says Ellen, a New York lab technician. "The thing is, fingerprints are mostly oils, and technically speaking, the oils that your fingers secrete could stay on a metal surface a long time. But really, in a lot of cases, if you have a gun that's been in a river with a swift current, or if the gun's become corroded, you aren't going to find any print worth recovering."[59]

Ellen says that she recently recovered a print found on an ammunition clip of a water gun. "That's the more likely place," she says.

Magazines, cartridges, ammunition clips—they're more protected than the surface of the gun, because they're inside the gun. In this case, divers had found the gun in shallow water in an irrigation ditch. It had been submerged less than twenty-four hours. We used what's basically a liquid fingerprint powder, that sprays onto the wet surface. It clings to the oils, and not the water, so you can come in later with sticky tape and lift the print, just as you would a print on a dry surface. In that case, it did work out for us, corroborating the statement of one of the men that it was the other guy who actually shot the gun, not him.[60]

But while fingerprints and other forensics tests are possible, crime lab technicians say that usually they send the gun

Steps in a Process: Fingerprinting a Submerged Weapon

1 First, make sure that the weapon has been kept in water since its recovery. Because fingerprints are mostly oils from the fingers, if the surface of the gun is allowed to dry, the oil will run and smudge.

2 Spray the surface of the weapon with a layer of a chemical called a Small Particle Reagent (SPR), which can fix the oily fingerprint in place.

3 Quickly spray the surface with water, which will rinse the SPR off. What is left is a visible fingerprint.

4 Apply a clear piece of sticky tape directly on the print and use a squeegee, running it across the tape, to push excess water away.

5 Carefully lift the tape (and with it, the fingerprint) and affix it to a plain white card. After using the squeegee once more to remove any water, a clear fingerprint will be ready to examine and compare with fingerprints of any known suspect—or to run through a computer fingerprint database.

to the firearms techs for ballistics testing. "The reason for that," says Ellen, "is that since the gun is going to corrode fast when we get it out of the water it's been transported in, it makes more sense to do the test that is absolutely the most likely to have results—and that's ballistics."[61]

"The Thing Was Pretty Disgusting"

One of the most important objects of ballistics testing is to find out if the gun is actually the one that fired the bullets in a shooting crime. The only way to do that is to compare the bullet removed from the body of the victim (or recovered from the scene) with another bullet that has been test-fired from that same gun. But to do that, the crime lab needs to get that weapon—often referred to by firearms analysts as a "water gun"—to work one more time. And that is no easy accomplishment, says Erica Henderson, a firearms analyst at Minnesota's Bureau of Criminal Apprehension (BCA).

"Water guns usually come to us in bad shape," she says.

> To get one to work again is a real challenge. If it's been down there awhile, the slide won't work, so you can't get to the cartridges inside to be able to recover them, to see what type of ammunition is in there. To get things moving again, the first thing you have to do is get the gun soaking in oil. That can slow down the corrosion process, too. Anyway, we use any kind of oil—WD-40, Rust-Off, whatever works that can get the parts moving again.[62]

Henderson says the soaking process requires patience. "It can be a long process," she says.

> I remember this one specialist worked on a gun for weeks and weeks. It was a long gun, a rifle. The stock—that's the part you put up against your shoulder when you fire it—was all rotted off, so she just had the metal portion. But the thing was pretty disgusting; it stunk, it was all full of barnacles. But as I said, she kept working on it, changing the oil, scrubbing it, gradually getting all of the gunk off it. You have to be really careful, too—you can't use anything abrasive that might scratch parts of the gun that will need for identification purposes, such as the serial number.[63]

Becoming a Firearms Analyst

Job Description:

The analyst must be able to conduct a series of tests on ammunition, using microscopes for comparisons. It is necessary to understand and recognize the differences between various types of firearms and be proficient at test firing them for comparisons. It is important to be able to use chemicals to enhance serial numbers on damaged weapons, too. A firearms analyst must be computer literate and able to use databases to discover whether a particular firearm has been used in other crimes. Finally, an analyst will occasionally be called upon to explain his or her findings to a jury.

Education:

Analysts must have a college degree with a science background. Most analysts today have strong backgrounds in chemistry or biology.

Salary:

Although salaries vary in different parts of the country, firearms specialists can begin at a salary of about $38,500, with experienced analysts making an annual salary of about $60,000.

A firearms analyst uses a microscope to compare markings on two bullets to determine if they match a gun used in a crime.

A forensics technician dusts a gun for fingerprints.

Test Fire

The firearms analyst's first goal is to get the gun into better condition so that forensic work on it can begin. One of the first things analysts do is find out whether that particular gun could be the one that was used to shoot the victim. Test-firing the gun is the best way to do that. The analyst fires the gun under controlled conditions and, in the case of a homicide investigation, compares the bullet with any bullets removed from the scene and/or the victim's body.

"Once the gun is in good enough condition that it can be fired and all the moving parts are working as they should, I need to remove any ammunition that might be in there," says Henderson. "Obviously I can't use it, because the gunpowder has gotten wet while it was underwater, so I go to the ammunitions closet here and get new bullets that are the type that were in the gun, if possible. I'll need two or three for my test fire—no more than that."[64]

If the gun is a handgun, it is test-fired in an 8-foot-long (2.4m) tank filled with water, about 4 feet (1.2m) deep. "The water in the tank puts up enough resistance to stop a bullet," says Henderson. "I fire the gun through a special opening at the side of the tank, and then I retrieve the bullets. We use a little suction hose afterwards to suck up the bullets from the bottom of the tank, to make the retrieval easy."[65]

However, if the water gun is a high-powered rifle, analysts do not use the water tank. Rifle bullets are so small, and are moving at such a high rate of speed, that the water in the tank would not stop them. In cases like these, the analyst uses a cotton box—a long box tightly filled with compressed cotton batting. Squares of corrugated cardboard are placed at 10-inch (25.4cm) intervals in the box. "They're called witness panels," explains Henderson. "They help when you have to go through all that cotton to find the bullet after you do the test fire. You

A police officer test-fires a gun inside a water tank. The bullet will be retrieved and analyzed wth microscopes and computers.

just find the last witness panel that's been penetrated [by the bullet] and you can at least narrow your search down. But it's still a pain . . . to search through that cotton for that bullet!"[66]

Class Characteristics, Individual Characteristics

Once the analyst has fired the water gun and retrieved the bullets, he or she needs to find out if they match the bullet recovered from the crime scene or the body of the victim. To do that, the analyst must first determine whether the bullets even came from the same type of gun.

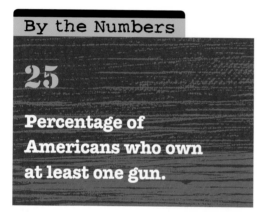

By the Numbers

25

Percentage of Americans who own at least one gun.

Figuring that out depends on detecting marks left on the bullet. A bullet, because of its oblong shape, needs to travel in a spiral, much like a thrown football. Experts know that inside the barrel of every handgun and rifle are marks. Some are intentional—put in by the manufacturer—and are called lands and grooves. The grooves spiral down the length of the barrel (the lands are ridges between the grooves), putting spin on the bullet to speed it more accurately to its target.

Not every gun has the same pattern of lands and grooves, nor are they made to spiral, or "twist," in the same direction. How many lands and grooves are in a particular gun, and which direction they twist, depends entirely on the manufacturer. For example, a Smith & Wesson gun is known for having five lands and grooves with a right twist. On the other hand, Colts have six lands and grooves with a left twist.

Bullets are almost always made of lead or copper, which are softer than the steel of a gun's barrel. As the lands and grooves grip the bullet and spin it as it goes through the barrel, the bullet picks up those marks. That is critically important information for firearms analysts, who can actually tell what sort of gun fired the bullet, based on those marks. Those marks will be found on every bullet that is shot from that type of gun—not just the murder weapon.

Under the Microscope

To view the bullets closely, the analyst uses an instrument called a comparison microscope. It is basically two microscopes connected by a bridge that contains a number of mirrors and lenses. This allows the analyst to view both the test-fired bullet and the crime scene bullet side by side.

"What I see is a circular area divided in half," says Henderson. "I'm looking at two bullets, one on each side. I can't get mixed up which is which, because I always make a little mark on each of my test fire bullets with an etching instrument, called a vibroscribe."[67]

A police forensics technician uses a comparison microscope (center) to compare a test-fired bullet with the crime scene bullet.

Looking through the microscope, the analysts can rotate the images and see the same view of each bullet. If they are a match, the lands and groove marks will be the same. "If that happens, I know they were fired by the same type of gun," Henderson explains. "It doesn't mean it was the same gun, though. At that point, I'm not able to say that—not yet, at least."[68]

"Accuracy Is Everything"

If the marks on the test-fired bullet show the same lands and groove marks as those on the crime scene bullet, the analyst proceeds to the next step. That means looking for "individual characteristics," formations within the barrel of a gun, specific only to that gun, and that would leave a specific mark on a bullet. Some weapons experts say that such characteristics are like a gun's DNA, for no two would have exactly the same marks in exactly the same place.

"It could be a mark left because there is some scratch inside the barrel, or maybe how the person cleaned that gun, which left a mark inside," says Henderson. "Or maybe there's some gunk in there that can also leave a mark on the bullet. It could be a manufacturing flaw, too—just some tiny imperfection that could leave a mark on the bullet that could only be seen under the microscope."[69]

Whatever caused the microscopic flaw that made a tiny mark on the bullet, says Henderson, is the evidence that allows her to say with confidence that that recovered gun is the right one. "As long as the same mark appears on both the test-fire bullet and the crime scene bullet at exactly the same place, you have a match," she says. "You really have to pay attention, because accuracy is everything. This comparison can prove that was the gun used in the crime."[70]

Chandler, who as a police diver helped find the two guns used in a double homicide, says that case hinged entirely on the bullets. "We had the vehicle that the bad guys drove, we had the bad guys themselves, but to put them in jail, we absolutely had to link those guns to the crime," he says. "So the lab did a test fire with both of the guns, and compared the characteristics of the bullets from the test fires with the bullets from the bodies of the victims, and so they were able to get a conclusive match. That let us go to court with proof that those guns were the ones that fired the shots that killed two people. That was really a good feeling to be able to verify that."[71]

The Reappearing Serial Number

But while proving that the recovered water gun was the one used to commit the murder is helpful, it does not necessarily tell investigators who pulled the trigger. Usually, tracing the weapon's serial number, which manufacturers stamp onto the frame of every gun, is a good place to start. When a gun is purchased legally, the serial number

By the Numbers

500,000

Number of guns reported stolen yearly in the United States.

is registered to the owner. Of course, a detective following the paper trail might learn that the gun's owner had nothing to do with the murder at all. Even so, says forensic expert D.P. Lyle, "he might have given the gun to someone, or it might have been stolen, and the murder and the gun theft could be linked. Comparing the evidence in the two cases would move the investigators closer to the perpetrator."[72]

However, it is often difficult or even impossible to read a serial number on a gun. In the saltwater of an ocean or in the strong current of a river, the numbers are likely to have been worn down, making them illegible. In some cases, the criminal may have purposely filed off the serial number to avoid detection. Even so, weapons analysts have ways to restore the numbers that may seem to have vanished altogether.

One good method is to apply a particular acid to the place on the gun's frame where the numbers used to be. That area of metal had been strained and compressed—and therefore

To retrieve a damaged serial number from a gun, a technician applies acids and other chemicals.

made more reactive to certain chemicals—when the manufacturer originally pressure-stamped those numbers into the gun. Those chemicals include etching acid.

After polishing the surface with a very fine-grit sandpaper, the analyst carefully applies acid to the area. The acid eats away the strained metal more quickly than the metal around it, and as that happens, the original number reappears. It is important to note that those numbers will not last long, for the acid will continue to damage the area. The analyst must photograph them quickly as proof of the serial number when the case goes to court.

Disappointment

But while recovered water guns can be crucial to solving a case, many times the gun is too badly damaged to be of use. "I think we've all had guns we've been unable to restore," says Henderson. "Sometimes you have one that you soak in every oil you can think of, work with it to try to get it so you can test-fire it, but you just can't get those moving parts to move. And without that test-fire, you've got nothing to compare with the recovered bullet."[73]

One case that disappointed investigators in Sweden had to do with a 1986 murder. Olof Palme, the prime minister of Sweden, was gunned down while walking to a theater with his wife. Police had a few leads, one of which was that the bullets recovered from the Palme crime scene were closely matched to bullets recovered from the scene of an armed robbery in the small town of Mockfjard, Sweden, in 1983. It seemed that the same gun likely fired both, but attempts to find the gun in nearby lakes were unsuccessful.

Then twenty years later, in 2006, following a confidential tip, divers searched again and this time found it. Roger Calsson, the crime lab's director, was doubtful that the gun could be test fired, saying the chances were "very small, not to say microscopic . . . if it has been in the water for that long."[74] Unfortunately for investigators, Calsson was right. Though police believed that it was the right gun, they had no way to prove it.

"It is too bad," says Allen, a Minnesota lab technician. "In the lab, you think about that a lot—like maybe if such and such a crime had only been committed a few years later, we'd be better able to figure it out [in the lab]. We see cases like that sometimes, where what we are capable of doing today isn't quite enough. But maybe when you look at the big picture, someday it will be—we'll be able to do those things and more."[75]

But even though occasional failures happen, weapons specialists are convinced that what they are able to do with firearms that have been submerged is valuable. Every day the information unlocked from those weapons is providing important clues that help convict criminals.

CHAPTER FOUR

The Problems with a Water Body

As tricky as it can be to collect evidence from water guns, however, no aspect of underwater forensics is harder than dealing with bodies that have been submerged. It is often impossible even to identify the body, let alone determine how the person died—by accident, suicide, or homicide. That is because bodies undergo very dramatic changes as they deteriorate in the water.

"River Bodies Are Difficult"

Michael McGee is the medical examiner for Ramsey County, Minnesota. He has examined hundreds of bodies that have either washed ashore or been recovered by divers. Many of those bodies are found in the deep, fast-moving Mississippi River, which flows right through the St. Paul metropolitan area.

"River bodies are difficult," he says. "They deteriorate, or break down, faster than a body on land, especially in warm water. And that means that you've got to have experience dealing with deteriorating bodies to be able to tell what changes are due to normal decomposition that takes place for any river body, and what might be due to trauma, or injuries that caused that person's death."[76]

The two most crucial jobs for the medical examiner are to identify the body and to establish how the person died. "The identification is most important," McGee stresses. "If you don't get them identified, you really can't go any further. Even if you learn that they've died from a gunshot wound, for

instance, or they were strangled, the case has nowhere to go until we know who that person was."[77]

Who Are You?

In some cases, especially if the body has not been submerged for too long, it might be possible to get fingerprints. The fingertips of a submerged body usually are misshapen and wrinkled from being in the water. A fingerprint technician can get good results by injecting the fingers with a liquid called "tissue builder." That solution can cause the fingertips to swell to a normal shape so they can be fingerprinted.

However, when the body has been submerged for weeks or months and has become bloated (gas from the body makes the tissues expand), the ridges that are the basis of all fingerprinting are very difficult to see. In these circumstances, the fingerprint technician can shine a bright light on the finger from a side angle. That way, the valleys—the spaces between the ridges—suddenly become more apparent as shadows. Instead of actually creating inked fingerprints, the technician can simply take a photograph of that pattern.

But even a good fingerprint is useless unless investigators have a print with which to compare it. Unless a person has a criminal record or has been in the armed forces, his or her fingerprints are not likely to be on file. So running a set of fingerprints through a computer database, no matter how complete, may not find a match.

Teeth Can Tell

On the other hand, most people have gone to a dentist, and if they have had dental X-rays, those records should be on file. Teeth have become one of the most helpful ways of verifying a body's identity. If the body's head is intact, the medical examiner will often depend on dental experts for help.

"They can either x-ray the teeth, much like a dentist would do for a living patient," says McGee,

> or we can remove the upper and lower jaw, and do a panoramic X-ray and chart [the teeth]. The dental expert will not only pay attention to fillings and crowns, which show up on X-rays, but also missing teeth and evidence of procedures like root canals. And if we have an idea of who the body might be, like if there is a missing persons report, we can follow through and have a dental record to compare with that of the missing person.[78]

Police divers in training participate in an underwater excercise to recover a body.

"It's Just a Fact of Life"

But while dental X-rays and fingerprinting can help identi-fy some water bodies, these procedures would be useless for many. Many bodies that have been submerged for a long time go through a process called disarticulation—certain parts of their bodies have separated at the joints. The most common body parts to be disarticulated are hands, ankles, and the head.

"When you think about it, it does kind of make sense," says McGee. "The neck is very small, once that tissue deteriorates. When that happens, the only thing that holds the head on is

The VENUS Project

Homicide investigators have always been puzzled by the changes that occur to a human body that has been submerged in water. For example, investigators of land homicides know that certain insect activity takes place at particular stages of decomposition, and know-ing about that activity has helped detectives narrow down a time of death. Scientists in British Columbia have begun a project that will help in water investigations. It is called the Victoria Experimental Network Under the Sea, or VENUS.

They do not use a human body but rather a pig carcass, since pigs' skin has most of the properties of human skin. They lower the carcass on a hook into deep water next to a camera set up on the ocean floor. Pictures and data about water temperature, oxygen levels, and so on, are transmitted back to the lab. Though it may seem gruesome to watch crabs, turtles, and starfish feeding on the body, scientists are learning a great deal. For instance, they know that marine life feeds on the face and head last, unlike land animals. Finding no marks on a body but dam-age to the face will suggest foul play.

the spinal column. And it's maybe not pleasant to think about, but it's a fact of life, that if there is fish activity, or the body comes into contact with an underwater object as it moves in a current—let's say it hits part of a tree underwater—it can just get bumped off." He adds that this is the same reason that hands and feet are often gone from a water body. "The only thing holding your hand on your arm is the attachment of tendons. Really, your wrist joint is just that, a joint. Your hand is not fused to your arm. Once the soft tissue is gone, it doesn't take much for it to fall out. And that is too bad, because that body is then without hands to fingerprint, and without a head to get dental ID. But the longer the body is in the water, the more parts it loses."[79]

By the Numbers

25

Percentage of American adults who have ever been fingerprinted.

Working with What You've Got

After noting the condition of the body and taking fingerprints or dental X-rays, if possible, the medical examiner begins by inspecting the outside of the body for tattoos or jewelry. Many people who have served in the armed services, for example, have had the name and number of their unit tattooed on their bodies.

Clothing, too, can sometimes provide clues to the identity of a body. In March 2009 a body was pulled from a canal in Yorkshire, England. At first it seemed that nothing provided a clue to its identity other than that the person was male and probably Asian. It seemed odd, too, that no one had reported a man missing. An examination of the body showed that the man had been severely beaten, tied to weights, and thrown into the canal. The man had no identification, however, and police were stumped.

Then one of the technicians noticed that the shirt on the body had a label. Further investigation found that the shirt had been made in China but not sold anywhere in Britain.

A victim's clothing can be a source of clues for forensic investigators.

Although as of July 2009 the case has not been solved, investigators believe that the man was probably being illegally trafficked into the country when he was killed.

Once the clothing has been searched for clues, the medical examiner thoroughly X-rays the body. That can be helpful for two reasons. The first is that a prosthetic device in the body—a pacemaker or an artificial hip, for example, might be found.

McGee says that in a recent case he saw an implanted spinal device in the X-ray of a body, and he was able to identify the body as a result:

> At the end of the autopsy, you can just saw it out, and at the base of the device is the name of the company that makes it, and a number. So you get on the phone and call United Orthotics from Chicago, or whatever the company is, and say, "Hey, can you guys check a number for me?" They look it up on their computer that such and such a doctor installed it on a certain date, and then you work backwards. Call the doctor, get the information—the name of the patient, phone number of a family member, whatever it is. In these kinds of situations, X-rays can be very, very helpful.[80]

Forensic investigators routinely X-ray bodies to aid them in their investigations.

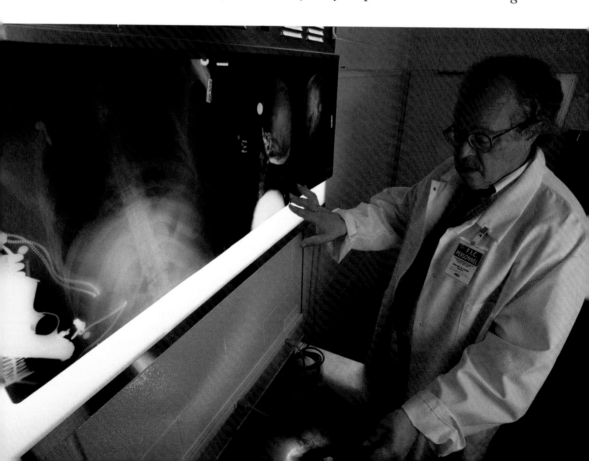

How Bones Can Help

The other way X-rays can help a medical examiner is by revealing fractures in a body's bones that might give some idea of who that person was. "If we have a missing persons report—let's say it was someone believed to have disappeared near the river—and divers have recovered a river body," says McGee, "and let's say we see on the report that the person had an old fracture, a broken wrist. Even though it has healed long ago, we should be able to see evidence on that X-ray to tell us that this could be a match."[81]

A device is used to measure a human mandible, the lower part of the jaw.

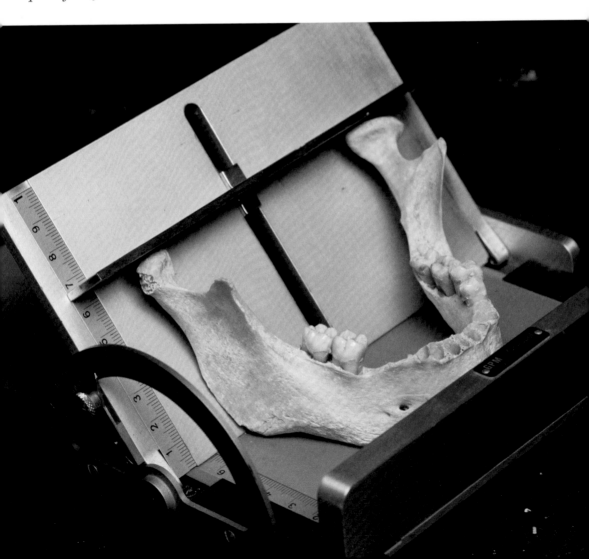

An X-ray actually identified the body in the Christine Elkins murder. Investigators finally found her car, with the aid of the magnetometer, at the bottom of the Missouri River. But though an informant had told the police that Elkins's killer had stuffed her body in the trunk of the car, only skeletal remains were recovered after so many years underwater. A dental match was discussed, because the jawbone and teeth were still intact. However, Elkins's dental records could not be located for a match.

Instead, the medical examiner hoped he could find a match with an X-ray. He had learned from Elkins's family that when she was younger, she had suffered a broken tailbone. At that time, she had been given a full-body X-ray, and those records were available. On these new X-rays, the medical examiner could clearly see evidence of the mended tailbone, as well as other characteristics that appeared on the old X-rays. That enabled investigators to say for certain that the body in the car was that of Christine Elkins, thus allowing police to officially charge drug dealer Tony Emery with her murder.

The Lack of an X-Ray

On the other hand, *not* taking an X-ray of a submerged body could be a huge mistake that lets a murderer go free. No better example of this can be found than the case of a fouteen-year-old Baraboo, Wisconsin, boy named Chris Steiner. On July 4, 1992, his parents called police when they found their son missing. Evidence suggested that he might have been abducted. His bedroom window screen had been sliced open, and muddy footprints were inside.

However, police were unable to find any trace of the teen until, five days later, his body was found washed up on a shallow sandbar in the Wisconsin River. The medical examiner did an autopsy but found no apparent wounds that would point to a homicide. The death was declared an accidental drowning. If it had not been for another event in Baraboo a year later, the strange case would never had been solved.

On July 29, 1995, thirteen-year-old Thad Phillips awoke in the middle of the night on the living room couch after falling asleep watching TV. He found himself being picked up from the living room couch and carried outside. Groggy with sleep, he stumbled along with his abductor, not understanding what was happening.

Breaking and Setting

His abductor was an older teen, seventeen-year-old Joe Clark. When Clark got Phillips to his home, he started torturing him, twisting bones in his ankles and upper legs until they broke. Afterward, Clark began setting Phillips's broken bones in crude casts made of ace bandages and old socks.

The next day, Phillips managed to get to a phone when Clark had left him alone. Delirious with pain, he called for help, and soon afterward Clark was arrested. Phillips told police that Clark had mentioned doing the same thing to two other boys, one of whom was named Chris. Wondering if that "Chris" was Chris Steiner, police had the boy's body exhumed, or recovered from his grave. The medical examiner took X-rays and found the same sorts of injuries to Steiner's ankles that Phillips had suffered. Likely, investigators believe, Clark was intending to dispose of Phillips's body in the river as he had done with Steiner's body. Experts realized that instead of an accidental drowning, it had actually been a murder.

DNA and Water Bodies

Another important tool in identifying a water body—especially a disarticulated body—is DNA. DNA contains genetic information unique to that individual and is found in the nuclei of the body's cells. "DNA is what is changing our role in identifying bodies," says McGee. "It's become easier and less expensive over the years, and no longer is it just done by one or two laboratories in the United States. Now we have DNA labs locally that can do the work relatively quickly."[82]

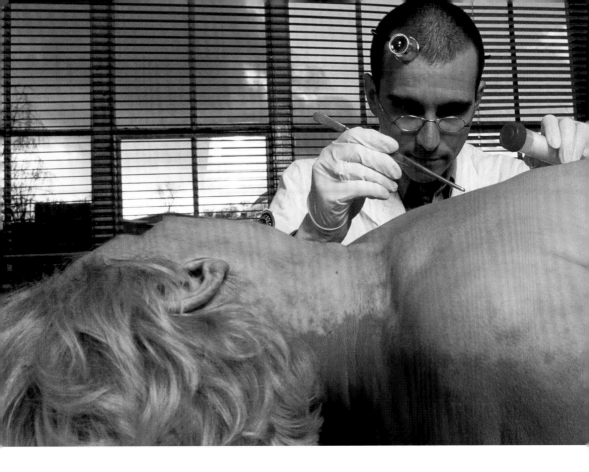

DNA helped identify the remains of a body of a teenage boy recently, says McGee. "He'd had a fight with his mother, and had taken off on his bike," he says. "She called the police, who found the bike by the water's edge, but they couldn't find him. Then, three months later, remains—including the boy's jacket—were found. But the remains were just a torso, nothing that would help us with an identification." McGee says that he asked the lab if they could identify it from DNA. "There wasn't much blood left, in this case," he explains. "And [blood] is usually what we sent [to the DNA lab] for testing. So we asked if they could get DNA from the tissue. And that's exactly what they did—they got it from bone marrow (material inside the bones). And that provided a positive identification of the missing boy."[83]

The news was certainly not a happy ending, admits McGee, but it did provide a definite answer to what became of the boy. "Sometimes, that's the best we can do,"[84] he says.

As a means of establishing positive identification, a forensic technician collects DNA from a drowning victim.

Looking for a Cause of Death

Once all means of identification have been used, the medical examiner begins looking for a cause of death. McGee says he starts with three main questions:

> I want to learn if there is any evidence of injury to the body—and if so, what? Any evidence of natural disease—if so, what? Any evidence of drugs onboard—if so, what? All of those questions can usually be answered, unless the body is extremely decomposed—and even then, we've been able to find ways to get the answers.[85]

Injury might mean that the person was attacked or beaten before he died. Chandler suspected that exact scenario when he was called to do a body recovery in the Mississippi River. "A guy reported to the cops that another guy had fallen into the water," he remembers. "I was talking to the witness—he was a transient, a homeless guy. But his story was a little weird—didn't make a lot of sense. And as I was talking with him, trying to get an account of where the guy had fallen, what had happened—I noticed that his hands were marked, like he'd maybe gotten into a fight and scuffed them up."[86]

Believing that the witness was actually responsible for the death, Chandler called detectives in, and they talked with him. "They got him to confess—it was his friend, they had gotten into a fight about drinking," says Chandler. "This guy—the witness—he punched the victim, who ended up in the water and drowned. And because they were friends, he felt bad about it and called it in. And so when they recovered the body—it was within two hours or so—you could see where he'd been punched. That was a relatively easy case."[87]

"That Means He Was Alive"

Sometimes the medical examiner finds wounds on the body that raise questions as to how they got there. "The thing is,"

Trace Evidence

Although it has not occurred often, sometimes trace evidence on a submerged body has been found and linked the body to a suspect. That was the case in a famous serial murder case in Atlanta, Georgia. Between 1979 and 1981, several young African American men had been strangled, and some of the bodies were dumped in a nearby river. Many of the victims had mysterious fibers still on their clothing—even on those bodies that had been recovered from the river.

Investigators traced the two types of fibers by their color and chemical makeup. One type of fiber was found to be from a carpet used in certain General Motors cars. The other was from a home carpet manu-

facturer that had produced a limited amount of that color and type. Detectives had a suspect—twenty-three-year-old Wayne Williams—and were able to match both fibers to carpeting in Williams's home, as well as in his vehicle. The probability of both matches with any other individual, police said, was about one in 30 million.

Atlanta child murderer Wayne Williams was convicted in 1982 on trace evidence fibers.

says McGee, "unless you have a witness, there is no proof that those wounds caused the person to fall into the water."[88] In fact, he says, he had a recent case where wounds were on the body, but he had no way to answer the question: Are those wounds part of the story of how that person ended up in the river?

"We had a guy out running along the river," says McGee, "and he sees what he thinks is a body. It's over near Harriet Island near where the houseboats are docked. Anyway, the guy calls the squad, and they come, they think it's a body, too. So they get the sheriff's water patrol, and they recover the body. It's a man, dead, fully clothed, but not badly decomposed. Who he is—we have no idea."[89]

McGee says that upon checking his clothing, they found a wallet. "Okay, so now we know who he is—we find out he's a drug dealer. We do a toxicology screen on the body—that's a way to test for drugs or alcohol levels in the blood. We find out he's got a great deal of cocaine in his system. And there are all these injuries on his body—bruises, abrasions, like he's been beat up."[90]

Marks on a submerged body can be important. Because medical examiners can tell whether they were made before death or if they occurred after death, the bruises can sometimes give police an idea of whether the person was the victim of a homicide. "What told us that he was alive at the time of the fight was that the injuries weren't only on the surface of the body," says McGee. "We found hemorrhaging [internal bleeding] in the soft tissue underneath. That means he was alive."[91]

"I Can't Do That"

But that is all it tells the examiner. Trying to say definitely what caused those injuries or who caused those injuries would be mere speculation. Investigators say that many television shows leave viewers with this misunderstanding—that a test or an instrument can definitely prove if someone has drowned by accident or was killed and pushed into the water. Not so, says McGee.

"There is a lot of discussion about exams that you can do on recovered water bodies to determine if they were dead or alive when they went in the water," he says. "All these different studies, but the bottom line is, there really aren't any that are very good. So, can I sit here and tell you absolutely that someone died because of drowning, or died and then fell into the water? No, I can't do that."[92]

What a medical examiner can do, he says, is provide scenarios that might be true. And the best way of telling which of these scenarios is the most likely cause of death is to learn more about the person's life. McGee recalls that Joe Davis, who used to be the medical examiner in Miami County, Florida, had a saying: "If you want to find out what happened to a dead person, get him identified, and then once you've done that, go

Investigators say that television shows such as CSI Las Vegas *(pictured) give viewers a false impression of the ease of solving crimes.*

ask his friends. And they'll tell you. In a few minutes," Davis would say, "you'll know a lot of information that will help you figure out how they got all those injuries."[93]

Two Stories

To illustrate that idea, McGee proposes two stories about the drug dealer submerged in the water. "You could look at it like this," he says. "Here's a guy who uses drugs, sells drugs, and when he used drugs he fell down a lot. And one day he was really depressed about being a drug abuse guy, so he threw himself in the water. That explains the injuries, and how he got in the water." The second story, he says, also explains the injuries and how he got into the water. "Here's a guy who owed his drug suppliers a lot of money. They were after him, and beat him up, and threw him into the river, where he drowned."[94]

Which story is true? In this case, as in many water deaths, the answer will not be found by the medical examiners or the toxicology lab, or even the divers who retrieved the body. The answer will probably be found by police asking the right questions of the right people—the people who knew the drug dealer as a living person rather than a body on a table in the medical examiner's office. As is true with other aspects of an underwater crime scene, the medical examiner's findings are only one piece of the puzzle—although a very valuable piece.

CHAPTER FIVE

Underwater Forensics and Catastrophes

Underwater forensics cannot only help police solve crimes, it can also assist in the investigation of plane crashes, the sinking of ships, and catastrophic explosions in or near water. In many such cases, the essential task for authorities is to learn whether terrorism played a role in the event. But even when terrorism has been ruled out, experts must identify the causes of these catastrophes in order to correct technical errors or malfunctions so they do not happen again.

The Explosion of Flight 800

One of the most thorough investigations in modern history involving an underwater catastrophe was that of TWA Flight 800. On July 18, 1996, the airliner, which was on its way to Paris, exploded over the Atlantic Ocean just twelve minutes after takeoff from New York's John F. Kennedy International Airport. All passengers and crew onboard—a total of 230 people—were killed in the explosion.

Getting answers was urgent because of the widely held theory that the explosion had been orchestrated by terrorists. The idea was certainly not out of the question, for Americans had been frequent targets of terrorism during that time. Just one month before, terrorists had used a truck bomb to kill nineteen American soldiers in Saudi Arabia. A month before the truck bombing, domestic terrorists had set off explosions that killed 168 people in Oklahoma City. And in 1988 terrorists had planted a bomb onboard TWA Flight 103. That explosion occurred over Scotland and resulted in the deaths of all 259 people onboard. So the possibility that the huge explosion of Flight 800 had been caused by a bomb onboard

Investigators on a coast guard cutter gather wreckage from TWA Flight 800, as part of the forensic investigation into the crash.

the plane was very real in people's minds, including the investigators.

Of course, other explanations were possible, too. Some believed that the tragedy had resulted from a mechanical malfunction. Others wondered if the pilots had made some error during the takeoff that resulted in the explosion. Another theory was that a nearby naval base had been firing test missiles and had mistakenly targeted the airliner. Besides mourning the deaths of the passengers and crew, many Americans were very nervous.

Recovery Only

The most important part of the mission was to answer the question: Why did this happen? As with all accidents in the United States involving airplanes, that job fell to the investigators of the National Transportation Safety Board, or NTSB. In addition, the NTSB would receive assistance from the FBI, the navy, the coast guard, and a host of forensic experts.

But another important—and very immediate—part of the mission was to find any victims of the crash who may have survived. However, as navy and coast guard ships combed through the areas where some floating debris had been discovered, no sign of life was found. The mission quickly became one of recovery only. Hundreds of families waited anxiously for word that their loved ones' bodies had been found.

However, it is not only bodies of the victims that must be recovered after catastrophes such as this one. Finding as much of the plane's wreckage as possible is crucial. By examining the pieces, forensic experts would try to figure out precisely where on the aircraft the explosion had occurred and what the cause of that explosion was. But in the choppy water of the Atlantic Ocean, locating the wreckage of Flight 800 was as difficult as finding the bodies of the victims.

By the Numbers

7,000

Number of interviews done by the FBI in the Flight 800 investigation.

Searching for a Place to Search

As is the case with most underwater forensic missions of this size, the investigation of Flight 800 could not begin until the scene of the crash was located. That is much harder than it sounds, because in an explosion of a plane in flight, the debris can be scattered over many miles of ocean. In this case, investigators knew that the plane had exploded at an altitude of about 13,700 feet (4.17km). They also knew that fifteen minutes after the explosion, debris was still showering down into the water—making recovery of the plane and bodies an extremely difficult job.

The coast guard first used seven large patrol boats, three planes, and a helicopter to move back and forth—called "mowing the lawn"—across the 75-mile (120.7km) area where most of the plane was believed to have gone down. They found floating debris—mostly insulation and floating seat cushions rather than the engine parts or other structural parts of the plane that would be helpful in determining the cause of the

A U.S Navy ship participates in the search for the crash site of Flight 800.

A U.S. Navy diver is shown on the ocean floor carefully working his way through the debris field of Flight 800.

crash. Bodies were difficult to locate at first, although one coast guard officer said that it was not surprising. Seeing a body floating in the ocean from an airplane, he says, "could be compared to finding a ping pong ball in an Olympic-sized swimming pool from 500 feet [152m] up."[95]

The weather did not help, either. For the first two days, fog and choppy seas made it difficult to see much at all on the surface of the water. Instead, the coast guard crews concentrated

As part of the search for Flight 800 many remotely operated vehicles (ROVs) were deployed over the search area.

on using side-scan sonar, just as police divers use—in this case hoping to find objects below the water that might be bodies or parts of the plane.

In addition to the side-scan sonar, the boats were equipped with ROVs, or remotely operated vehicles. These robotic instruments are operated by crew members on the boat and can be sent into areas that are either too deep or too dangerous for divers. "The beauty of ROVs," says sonar expert Tom Vlesk, "is they're equipped with huge floodlights and cameras, so up top we can get pictures of any targets our sonar picks up. That way you don't send divers down unless there's something there."[96]

Chasing Pings

The acoustic sensor is another instrument useful in underwater investigations of plane crashes. It is used to help crews locate two of the most important parts of any aircraft—what

Not Black, but Orange

Neither of an airplane's black boxes is black at all. Both are painted glow-in-the-dark orange, so if a plane crashes on land, searchers would be able to find them more easily. Of course, in an underwater search such as that for Flight 800, the water would be too dark for any color to be of help. The "black" part of the term actually means that its information is confidential. If the cockpit voice recorder was played back publicly and an argument had occurred between the pilots during a crisis, for example, it could be embarrassing to families or coworkers. That is why only the investigators listen to it.

NTSB investigators show members of the media the black boxes recovered from Flight 800.

are known as "black boxes." The first box is the flight data recorder, or FDR, which automatically records every piece of data from the airplane as it is in the air—speed, altitude, which switches were on or off at any given time—and more than a thousand other bits of information. Having the FDR is key for forensic investigators. By programming the settings of each part of the airplane into a computer, they may be able to create a "virtual reality" that allows them to see precisely what was happening in the moments before the plane exploded.

The second black box is the cockpit voice recorder, or CVR. That instrument records everything that is said between the pilot and copilot in the cockpit. By listening to those recordings, investigators might hear a remark, for instance, that they had seen something odd, or maybe a comment about some instrument that was not functioning.

The black boxes are designed to emit an electronic pinging sound after a crash to enable recovery workers to find them. The acoustic sensors onboard the boats are so sensitive that they can "listen" more than 20,000 feet (6,100m) below the water for the ping. It is important for crews to find the boxes fast, however, for the pings go on for only about a month.

Hard Hat Divers

As the boats made their sweeps with sonar and ROVs, officials were gradually able to reduce the area in which most of Flight 800's wreckage would likely be found. Each morning, divers were taken to areas where ROVs had taken both still photos and video of targets most likely to be bodies or pieces of the aircraft.

In the first hours after the explosion, local police divers—including those from the NYPD—were used. However, they were unequipped to stay very long on the ocean floor. It took time for them to descend 130 feet (39.6m), and since they also had to resurface very slowly to avoid decompression sickness, their working time was about ten minutes. That is because the

46ºF (7.7ºC) water temperature made it necessary to limit total diving time to an hour.

Within a week of the explosion, however, navy divers were brought in on a ship called the *Grasp*, specifically built for recovery of sunken ships or other salvaging operations. Called "hard hat divers," they specialize in deepwater diving and get their name from the large hard helmet they wear. Rather than carry air tanks on their backs, each diver wore a 30-pound (13.6kg) helmet with a hose that supplied him with an air mixture specially formulated for deep dives. The *Grasp* also speeded up the process of descending to the ocean floor and of coming up again. It has a metal platform that lowered a two-person team down to the bottom. When their time was up, the platform could be raised quickly. Decompression sickness was not a worry, for the ship was equipped with a special decompression chamber that the divers entered upon resurfacing.

By the Numbers

$5 MILLION

Price of a large ROV used for deepwater investigations.

Diving in "Mako City"

Just as police divers searching for forensic evidence at a crime scene encounter dangers, the navy divers did, too. The waters in which they did much of their diving were home to large numbers of medium-sized sharks, known as makos. The divers nervously dubbed their frigid water habitat "Mako City" as they began the slow process of recovering victims and parts of the plane.

It was eerily still, cold, and, except for the headlamps they wore, very dark as they made their descent to the scene. Said one diver, "We're talking of an 11- or 12-story building—that's the depth you've got to go down. You're floating in the darkness. You can't see anything. I just heard my own regulator, my own bubbles. All of a sudden, the bottom just comes out of the blackness, and then you start your search."[97]

What struck divers after making the descent to the bottom was the sheer size and scope of the scene. The airplane was in a lot of pieces, ranging from huge 30- by 60-foot (9.14m by 18.28m) chunks of the fuselage to tiny pieces that a diver could hold in his palm. Razor-sharp edges of the plane, electrical wires, and other obstacles were an ever-present danger. To navy diver David Loring it looked as though "you took a junkyard and threw it in water."[98]

They worked in pairs, unlike most police dives. One of the divers would use a video camera to document the position of the pieces of wreckage before they set to work retrieving them. The smaller pieces were put in a basket on the platform. In the case of larger sections, divers placed thick nylon cords around them (often with the help of the ROV), and the *Grasp* would use its cranes to pull them up. Bodies—or parts of bodies—were placed on the metal platform to be brought to the surface, too. The work was methodical and slow, and after working their hour shift, divers would ascend to the ship. A new team would then take their place on the bottom.

The massive destruction and loss of life was emotionally difficult for many of the divers. Some met with counselors to talk about what they had been experiencing. Diving supervisors said their divers were seeing things that none of them had ever seen before. One diver agreed, saying, "Nothing compares to this. I hope nothing in my life will compare with this."[99]

By the Numbers

240

Number of divers who worked the Flight 800 underwater investigation.

Recovery and Beyond

The recovered bodies were taken by boats from the *Grasp* to a makeshift command post where they were loaded onto refrigerated trucks and moved to the county medical examiner's office. Unlike most criminal investigations where the cause of death is often uncertain, the victims of Flight 800 were not autopsied. Instead, they were examined to try to establish identification. Most victims were identified by means of dental records provided by their families.

It was the wreckage of the plane, on the other hand, that would yield the most important clues about the cause of the explosion. Working around the clock, divers had found more than 70 percent of the wreckage by the end of September 1996. After that, the navy used special boats used in scallop fishing to trawl the area for any remaining pieces—a job that took several months. By the end of that time, NTSB officials estimated that nearly 95 percent of the wreckage had been located.

Members of a U.S. Navy dive team prepare for a dive to recover the bodies of victims from downed Flight 800. Some divers required counseling to help them cope with the grim search.

As the recovery of the wreckage was going on, trucks were carefully moving the pieces to an empty airplane hangar on Long Island. It is here that the forensic experts would begin their analysis of the wreckage to see what clues, if any, would tell them what had caused the crash.

The wreckage of Flight 800 is laid out in an aircraft hanger, where NTSB investigators try to piece together what happened to the plane.

"One of the World's Biggest . . . Jigsaw Puzzles"

To do that, investigators at the NTSB labeled each piece and laid it out with others that would be near it in the airplane. Then they attempted to actually put the plane back together, in what Larry Jackson of the NTSB calls "one of the world's biggest and heaviest jigsaw puzzles."[100]

By referring to microfilm containing the elaborate blueprints for the large airliner, investigators could find out where a particular little piece was supposed to go. Large pieces, on the other hand, are stamped every 20 inches (50.8cm) by manufacturers, so it was much easier to figure out where they belonged. Bit by bit the plane was reconstructed so that forensic experts could get a sense of where the explosion occurred.

Interestingly, the sonar images, the ROV photographs, and the video shot by divers themselves can be very important to the forensic experts, too. In the case of Flight 800, investigators studied the position of the pieces of wreckage on the ocean floor and believed they could determine the order in which the parts came off the plane when it exploded.

While heavier pieces such as landing gear will almost always sink right to the bottom, many of the lighter pieces can be carried by wind or current. By doing research on the air speed and current at the time of the explosion, experts can plot out—with surprising accuracy—the likely sequence of how those parts landed in the water.

Under the Microscope

Metallurgists, experts on the properties of metal and how it shows damages or breaks, were key to this part of the investigation. The metallurgist uses a special instrument called a scanning acoustic microscope (SAM), which uses sound waves rather than light to get a close-up image of metal.

By focusing on a particular area of interest, the SAM bombards the metal with sound waves that can give the investigator a detailed view of the surface, showing the shape and size of the tiniest crack or other damage. Experts say a crack resulting from years of use—called a fatigue crack—definitely looks different from the damage caused by a sudden event, such as a bomb.

"If you were to look at the part under very high magnification, you could see these little ripples, and that's where the . . .

crack has slowly grown as it fatigued," says Tom Haueter. On the other hand, he says, a break in metal from a bomb would show no ripples. "It doesn't look like that at all," he says. "It's just all of a sudden, the metal's just ripped, and it has a very similar surface all the way across."[101]

Never Mind

One of the key parts of the investigation of the wreckage was testing for traces of explosives. If found, those traces could prove that a bomb caused the explosion. Forensic chemists have several ways of detecting traces of chemicals like explosives. One is to use a wet swab to take a sample of a piece of wreckage and study its chemical components. And when doing so, experts found something startling.

Studying the results of swabs from part of the passenger section and the rear cargo area, they found two strong traces of explosives—PETN and RDX. Both of these chemicals are used in making powerful plastic explosives, which had been used in other terrorist bombings around the world. Just when some investigators were ready to announce that they had found evidence of a bomb onboard, everything changed.

Police learned that that plane had been used just a week before in a K-9 police training exercise. Officers had placed packets of explosive ingredients in various parts of the airplane for their dogs to sniff out. Those ingredients included PETN and RDX. But with the information about the K-9 training, one investigator said, "This discovery would definitely hurt any attempt to build a . . . case of a bomb."[102]

"A Fatal Spark"

In the end, the criminal investigation of Flight 800 was able to eliminate terrorism as a cause of the explosion. The discovery of the black boxes had yielded no evidence pointing to a bomb nor had the examination of the metal fragments of the plane.

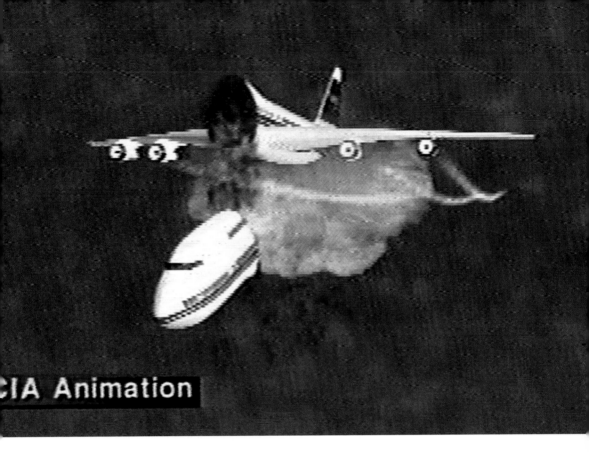

CIA Animation

No longer focusing on the bomb theory, investigators looked for a mechanical explanation—and eventually found one. The plane, the NTSB investigators found, had been destroyed by an explosion in a fuel tank. The tank had been almost empty—in fact, only vapors were inside. The "spark" that caused the explosion in the tank was found to be a wire above the tank, says underwater forensics expert Peter Limburg. "[The wire] had been damaged by repair work done at various times on the plane," he says, "and there was evidence of metal drill shavings in the hollow places inside the aircraft structure. This debris could have chafed the wiring . . . permitting a fatal spark."[103]

The NTSB released an animated film of the explosion on Flight 800.

"It Just Happens, and It's Frustrating"

The investigation of the explosion of Flight 800 shows how painstaking and thorough a process involving underwater forensics can be—and how helpful. But while law enforcement

Air France Bodies

A recent air disaster is that of Air France Flight 447. After taking off from Rio de Janeiro, Brazil, on its way to Paris on May 31, 2009, it crashed over the Atlantic Ocean, killing all 228 people on board. Because of the very deep waters, only a few bodies and a few pieces of the plane were recovered. The black boxes were not recovered, so forensic workers had very little to examine.

However, it was the condition of those bodies that led experts to feel confident that no explosion had occurred, for no burn marks were on bodies or plane debris. Nor had the plane crashed into the water. Instead, experts believe (as of July 2009) that the plane broke apart in midair, most likely due to a mechanical problem. An even bigger clue was that the bodies were whole—which would not have been likely had there been an explosion. Even more telling was the number of broken bones. "Typically," explained one forensic examiner, "if you see intact bodies and multiple fractures—arm, leg, hip fractures—it's a good indicator of a mid-flight break up."

Quoted in Stan Lehman and Emma Vandore, "Autopsies Suggest Air France Jet Broke Up in Sky," MSNBC, June 17, 2009. www.msnbc.msn.com/id/31410033/ns/world_news-americas.

agencies often rely heavily on science for testing and sampling of evidence, they are quick to point out that underwater criminal investigation is still fairly new in its development. The answer seems so close but ends up being just out of reach.

Experts point to the Laci Peterson case, in which the bodies of a young pregnant woman and her unborn child were found washed up onshore along the San Francisco Bay near Berkeley, California. Her husband was convicted of the murders not on the evidence from underwater forensics but rather by his own behavior. Though the two bodies could be positively identified, forensic experts were unable to say with any certainty either what the cause of death had been or who was responsible.

"We [divers] can recover the evidence they need, we can get exact measurements of what we've found, and we can give the investigators all the information we have, but it isn't always enough," says Hagen. "You know, like anything else, we are going to have cases that go nowhere. Maybe the gun we pulled out of the river won't fire in the ballistics lab to show a match, or the body can't be positively ID'd because it's too decomposed, or whatever. It just happens."[104]

Craig agrees but adds that new developments happen all the time that help investigators be more successful. "They're working with nano particles now that are going to make it easier to get prints from guns and other evidence—even stuff that's been underwater for years," he says. "Plus our diving gear and equipment is getting better all the time, so the next generation of divers is going to be able to do more, dive longer, and be safer. People need to remember it's a whole different world down there underwater. [It's a] perfect setup for a bad guy, right? Dark, mysterious."[105]

But thanks to the people who work with underwater evidence to solve crimes, those waters are getting less mysterious every day.

Notes

Introduction: "Everything's Different Now"

1. Dick Hagen, personal interview by author, Edina, Minnesota, April 10, 2009.

2. Dave, telephone interview by author, April 23, 2009.

3. Dave, telephone interview.

4. Quoted in FSU.com, "USCI: Underwater Crime Scene Identification." www.fsu.com/pages/2003/10/1/ucsi .html.

5. Don, telephone interview by author, April 24, 2009.

6. Hagen, interview.

7. Ron, personal interview by author, St. Paul, Minnesota, May 1, 2009.

Chapter One: "Cops with Swim Fins"

8. Tony, telephone interview by author, June 13, 2009.

9. Tony, telephone interview.

10. Hagen, personal interview.

11. Craig, telephone interview by author, June 18, 2009.

12. Quoted in Patrick Sweeney, "Divers Proceed 'By Braille,'" WTOV9, August 3, 2007. www.wtov9.com/news/13816258/detail.html.

13. Hagen, personal interview.

14. Hagen, personal interview.

15. Hagen, personal interview.

16. Al Rogers, telephone interview by author, June 13, 2009.

17. Rogers, telephone interview.

18. Hagen, personal interview.

19. Hagen, personal interview.

20. Hagen, personal interview.

21. Hagen, personal interview.

22. Hagen, personal interview.

23. Hagen, personal interview.

24. Hagen, personal interview.

25. Hagen, personal interview.

26. Craig, telephone interview.

27. Hagen, personal interview.

28. Craig, telephone interview.

29. Quoted in London Times Online, "A Life in the Day: Marion Dutton, Police Diver," January 4, 2009. www .timesonline.co.uk.tol.news/uk/crime/articles5434139.ece.

30. Quoted in London Times Online, "A Life in the Day: Marion Dutton, Police Diver."

31. Quoted in Nancy Gibbs, "Death and Deceit," *Time*, November 14, 1994. www.time.com/time/magazine/article/0,9171,981783-3,00.html.

32. Hagen, personal interview.

33. Hagen, personal interview.

34. Bill Chandler, personal interview by author, St. Paul, Minnesota, May 7, 2009.

35. Chandler, personal interview.

36. Chandler, personal interview.

Chapter Two: Finding the Underwater Evidence

37. Doug, telephone interview by author, May 1, 2009.

38. Doug, telephone interview.

39. Doug, telephone interview.

40. Quoted in Joe Cocozza, "New York Police Department: Scuba Team," 2002. http://homepage.mac.com/josephcocozza/poddiver/page18/page17.html.

41. Paul Hesson, telephone interview by author, May 11, 2009.

42. Hesson, telephone interview.

43. Hesson, telephone interview.

44. Jon Corbett, personal interview by author, Minneapolis, MN, June 8, 2009.

45. Hagen, personal interview.

46. Craig, telephone interview.

47. Chandler, personal interview.

48. Chandler, personal interview.

49. Chandler, personal interview.

50. Quoted in Steve Jackson, *No Stone Unturned: The Story of NecroSearch International.* New York: Kensington, 2002, p. 332.

51. Quoted in Jackson, *No Stone Unturned*, p. 333.

52. Ellen, telephone interview by author, May 21, 2009.

Chapter Three: Clues from a Water Gun

53. Craig, telephone interview.

54. Craig, telephone interview.

55. Hagen, personal interview.

56. Hagen, personal interview.

57. Chandler, personal interview.

58. Hagen, personal interview.

59. Ellen, telephone interview.

60. Ellen, telephone interview.

61. Ellen, telephone interview.

62. Erica Henderson, personal interview, St. Paul, Minnesota, April 17, 2009.

63. Henderson, personal interview.

64. Henderson, personal interview.

65. Henderson, personal interview.

66. Henderson, personal interview.

67. Henderson, personal interview.

68. Henderson, personal interview.

69. Henderson, personal interview.

70. Henderson, personal interview.

71. Chandler, personal interview.

72. D.P. Lyle, Forensics: *A Guide for Writers*. Cincinnati: Writer's Digest, 2009, p. 335.

73. Henderson, personal interview.

74. Quoted in "Handgun Recovered in Sweden Could Be Key to Palme Murder," November 21, 2006, FoxNews.com. http://origin.foxnews.com/story/92933,231077,00.html

75. Allen, personal interview, Minneapolis, Minnesota, June 22, 2009.

Chapter Four: The Problems with a Water Body

76. Michael McGee, personal interview with author, St. Paul, Minnesota, June 4, 2009.

77. McGee, personal interview.

78. McGee, personal interview.

79. McGee, personal interview.

80. McGee, personal interview.

81. McGee, personal interview.

82. McGee, personal interview.

83. McGee, personal interview.

84. McGee, personal interview.

85. McGee, personal interview.

86. Chandler, personal interview.

87. Chandler, personal interview.

88. McGee, personal interview.

89. McGee, personal interview.

90. McGee, personal interview.

91. McGee, personal interview.

92. McGee, personal interview.

93. McGee, personal interview.

94. McGee, personal interview.

Chapter Five: Underwater Forensics and Catastrophes

95. Quoted in Matthew W. Purdy, "The Crash of Flight 800: The Investigation," July 21, 1996, New York Times Online. www.nytimes.com/1996/07/21/nyregion/crash-flight-800-investigation-search-for-clues-flight-800-focuses-ocean-floor.html.

96. Tom Vlesk, telephone interview by author, July 1, 2009.

97. Quoted in Dan Barry, "Scouring a Cold, Dim Ocean Floor," New York Times Online, July 26, 1996. www.nytimes.com/1996/07/24/nyregion/fate-flight-800-divers-underwater-search-demands-skill-willingness-take-risks.html.

98. Quoted in Dan Barry, "Slow Walk with Danger in a Cold, Dim Junkyard," New York Times Online, July 31, 1996. www.nytimes.com/1996/07/31/nyregion/fate-of-flight-800-the-divers-slow-walk-with-danger-in-a-cold-dim-junkyard.html.

99. Quoted in Barry, "Scouring a Cold, Dim Ocean Floor."

100. Quoted in All Things Considered, "Analysis: Reconstruction of TWA Flight 800 Project," NPR, August 30, 1996, p. 1.

101. Quoted in All Things Considered, "NTSB Investigator Discusses TWA Flight 800 Crash," NPR, July 20, 1996, p. 1.

102. Quoted in Kevin Fedarko, "A Theory Gone to the Dogs," *Time*, September 30, 1996, p. 32.

103. Peter R. Limburg, *Deep-Sea Detectives: Maritime Mysteries and Forensic Science*. Toronto, ON: ECW, 2004, p. 199.

104. Hagen, personal interview.

105. Craig, telephone interview.

Glossary

autopsy: A medical examination of a dead body.

black boxes: The data recorder of an airplane and the cockpit recorder, which records everything said between the pilot and co-pilot.

decomposition: The breaking down of a body after death.

disarticulation: The separation of parts of a submerged body, such as head and hands.

exhume: To recover a body from a grave.

lands and grooves: The pattern of ridges and valleys inside the barrel of a firearm.

magnetometer: An instrument that can locate large metal objects underwater.

metallurgist: A person who specializes in the composition of various metals.

oxidation: Corrosion, or rusting, of metal.

plea bargain: A deal worked out between police and a suspect in which the suspect receives a more lenient sentence by cooperating with the police investigation.

public safety diver: Another term for police diver.

tender: The person holding on to the line connected to a diver.

For More Information

Books

ARDA (American Rescue Dog Association), *Search and Rescue Dogs: Training the K-9 Hero*. New York: Wiley, 2002. A detailed and highly readable book on training a dog for cadaver work.

Belinda Friedrich, *The Explosion of TWA Flight 800*. Philadelphia: Chelsea House, 2002. A good overview of the catastrophe, as well as the early theories about what caused it.

Walt "Butch" Hendrick and Andrea Zaferes, *Public Safety Diving*. Saddle Brook, NJ: Fire Engineering, 2000. Excellent information on equipment and strategies of searching for weapons or submerged bodies.

Periodicals

Edward Cody, "Air France Jet Was Intact Before Crash, Reports Say," *Boston Globe*, July 3, 2009.

Bridget Murphy, "A Unique Team of Forensic Divers from Florida State University Search for Natalee Holloway," *Florida Times Union*, July 27, 2005.

Internet Sources

Mary Calvi, "Underwater with FBI Divers," CBS, November 16, 2005. wcbstv.com/topstories/FBI.Divers.Scuba.2.231307.html.

Web Sites

Diving Health and Safety (www.Undercurrent.org/DivingMagazine). A wealth of interesting links to articles about some of the inherent dangers divers face, including decompression sickness, shark attacks, and accidents of all kinds.

Federal Bureau of Investigation (www.fbi.gov/hq/lab/html/ftu1.htm). The FBI's Web site includes links to information about the work of fingerprint and weapons analysts, as well as the contribution FBI divers make to important catastrophe investigations.

The Flight 800 Investigation (http://twa800.com). This site was created by retired military, civilian, and aviation experts who feel that the crash was not adequately solved by the NTSB and others. The site offers many articles about the initial investigation, with commentary pointing out questions that still remain.

TruTV "Underwater Forensics" (www .trutv.com/library/crime/criminal_mind/ forensics/underwater_forensics/1_index. html). This site has eleven subheads, including information on real cases in which underwater forensics played a key role, including the Laci Peterson murder and the Susan Smith case.

Index

Picture Credits

About the Author

Gail B. Stewart is the author of more than 240 books for children and teens. She is the mother of three grown sons and lives with her husband in Minneapolis.